LENDING POLICY
IF YOU DAMAGE OR LOSE THIS BOOK YOU
WILL ...
FAILU...
TRANSCRIPTS, AND LIBRARY PRIVILEGES.

DISCARD

S0-ATA-079

HV
3177
.C2
C25
1994

970547

Drawing strength
from diversity :
effective services
for children,
youth and families

DE 10 97

PERALTA COMMUNITY COLLEGE DISTRICT
Laney College Library
900 Fallon Street
Oakland, CA 94607

DISCARD

DEMCO

DISCARD

Drawing Strength from Diversity

◆

Effective Services for Children, Youth and Families

A California Tomorrow Research and Policy Report
From the Collaborative Services for Diverse Communities Project

By

Hedy Nai-Lin Chang, Project Director

Denise De La Rosa Salazar
Cecelia Leong

CALIFORNIA
TOMORROW

Board of Directors

Lewis H. Butler, Chair
Lily Wong Fillmore
Robert Friedman
Bong Hwan Kim
Martin Krasney
Stewart Kwoh
Antonia Lopez
Hugo Morales
Joyce Germaine Watts

Co-Directors

Laurie Olsen
Hedy Nai-Lin Chang

Staff and Project
Affiliates

Nancy Belton
Denise De La Rosa Salazar
Cecelia Leong
May Li
Zaida McCall Perez
Gregory McClain
Amy Muckelroy
Dora Maria Pulido
Lisa Raffel

CALIFORNIA TOMORROW is a non-profit organization committed to making racial and ethnic diversity work in California, and to building a society that is fair and open for everyone, especially for the children and youth who are our future.

CALIFORNIA TOMORROW

- Identifies and reports on the joys, challenges and problems that diversity brings to institutions serving children and their families.

- Seeks out and reports on the people and programs that deal most successfully with those challenges, and that build on the strengths of diversity.

- Delivers this news through publications and presentations to a broad cross-section of people.

- Brings outstanding community leaders and professionals together to share their experiences and perspectives on the challenges of a diverse California.

- Provides one-on-one consultation and assistance to agencies, schools and policymakers striving to create services and institutions appropriate to the rich diversity of our peoples.

- Through the media and other public forums, offers informed analysis of diversity issues in California, both the challenges and the successes, to counteract public ignorance, skepticism and fear.

CALIFORNIA TOMORROW
Fort Mason Center, Building B
San Francisco, CA 94123
(415) 441-7631

Drawing Strength From Diversity:
Effective Services for Children, Youth and Families

Editor: Katherine Kam

Design and Production: Alison Wood, Woodland Graphics

Cover photograph by Ted Scott III: Staff and children at New Helvetia Housing Project

Photographs on pages 5, 8, 45, and 65 were taken by Ted Scott III. All Rights Reserved

Photographs on pages 16, 27, 33, 43, 62 and 91 were taken by Cecelia Leong

Photograph on page 87 used with permission of the Vaughn Family Center

Funding for the Collaborative Services for Diverse Communities Project and for this publication was generously provided by:

The Annie E. Casey Foundation

The Stuart Foundations

The Pacific Mutual Foundation

Copyright © 1994 CALIFORNIA TOMORROW
All rights reserved
No part of this book may be reproduced without permission.

Contents

970547

ACKNOWLEDGMENTS

First and foremost, co-authors Cecelia Leong and Denise De La Rosa Salazar deserve thanks for pouring their dedication, talents, and hard work into this project. From the beginning, Cecelia has been instrumental in shaping the scope and depth of this work. She was invaluable for her ability to synthesize information — whether it be about outcomes or governance — while maintaining an eye toward specifics. An organizer *par excellence*, Cecelia deserves special recognition for managing the development, dissemination and analysis of the collaborative survey. She always made sure we never lost a project file or paper. Denise, who joined us soon after the project started, helped to ground us in the politics of community-based organizations and in the importance of building the capacity of community members to be active decision-makers. Denise also assumed primary responsibility for the literature review. This report truly bears the mark of both these colleagues' ideas and inspiration. I will never forget their willingness to spend day after day writing and revising various chapters to ensure that we achieved a coherent voice and a clear message.

Other California Tomorrow staff and consultants were also instrumental to the development of this work. As with any California Tomorrow activity, this project drew upon the wisdom and vision of Co-director Laurie Olsen. A careful and critical reviewer of every draft, Laurie constantly forced the project team to be clear about our assumptions and precise in our thinking. Project Associate Greg McClain was also an important member of the research team. Gifted with strong interpersonal and inter-viewing skills, Greg participated in several site visits, helped to facilitate the project retreat and reviewed the draft report. Consultant Laura Sakai undertook the painstaking task of crunching the data from the collaborative survey after it was carefully entered into database form by Avon Leong, who is greatly appreciated for his willingness to fill in during times of need. Editor Katherine Kam deserves special thanks for taking on the mammoth task of editing the final draft. A talented journalist, she took final responsibility for ensuring both flow and readability. Finally, I would like to acknowledge the contributions of our office staff, Nancy Belton and May Li. Ever patient and helpful, their support kept all of us moving ahead.

On behalf of the entire project team, I would also like to express our sincere appreciation to all the individuals who participated in our project retreat: Ann Alton, Connie Busse, Maria Casey, Judy Chynoweth, Zoe Clayson, Soraya Coley, Edith Crigler, Ray Colmenar, Ira Cutler, Sid Gardner, Beth Hart, Art Himmelman, Dick Loveall, Lisa Potter, Mitchell Salazar, Ted Scott, Ralph Smith, Lourdes Sullivan, Yoland Trevino, Lucy Trujillo, Joanna Uribe De Mena, and Sylvia Yee. Their extraordinary experience, knowledge and passion significantly broadened and deepened the scope of the research and the content of this report. Much to our delight, we were also able to draw upon the artistic abilities of retreat participant, Ted Scott, who took time out of his busy schedule to take photographs for the report. The cover picture is an illustration of his creative talents.

The more than fifty individuals who reviewed our initial draft deserve a special note of gratitude. These individuals include retreat participants, California Tomorrow staff and Board of Directors, as well as individuals from across the nation who are actively involved in improving services to children and families. Taking time out of their busy schedules to review our manuscript of more than 100 pages, these readers gave critical, constructive feedback about the tone and substance of our work. It is our hope that this review process will be the beginning of an on-going dialogue about the implications of diversity for the movement to reform services for children and families.

The Annie E. Casey Foundation provided major support for the development, production, and dissemination of this report. We would also like to thank the Stuart Foundations and the Pacific Mutual Foundation for their contributions. In addition to the appreciated monetary support, California Tomorrow also valued the willingness of staff at the Stuart and Casey foundations (Ted Lobman, Amy Loomis, Lisa Potter, and Ira Cutler) to engage in in-depth discussions about the substance and direction of this work.

Last, but certainly not least, thanks to all of the individuals who took the time out of their busy schedules to share their experiences and insights — whether by filling out a survey or taking part in an interview. It is their collective wisdom that forms the foundation of this report.

Hedy Nai-Lin Chang
Project Director

INTRODUCTION

S ix years ago, a mentally disturbed man with a history of hatred toward Asians fired 106 bullets into a Stockton, California, elementary schoolyard filled with Southeast Asian children. He killed five and wounded 29. The school's Cambodian and Vietnamese families, many who had fled the specter of war in their native countries, felt traumatized. Parents pulled their youngsters out of class. The state's normally fragmented mental health system attempted to respond quickly with counseling for the distraught families — only to find resistance to their well-intentioned efforts. Among Southeast Asians, someone is typically considered "crazy" or "normal," with no shades between. A person only seeks help from outsiders if s/he is insane. As the cultural complexities became more obvious, mental health and school professionals were forced to expand their view of mental health services beyond traditional western approaches. Eventually, these service providers learned from parents that allowing local Buddhist monks to hold a purification ceremony on the school grounds would help to restore a degree of emotional order. After the ritual, Southeast Asian families finally began to send their children back to classes.

· · · · · · · · · · · · · · · · ·

A Latina director headed a service integration effort that provided young families with a comprehensive array of support services. She planned to assign a Latino male worker the job of transporting mothers to the center, since many did not drive. Although the director shared the same ethnicity as many of the families targeted by the center, she had grown up in a middle-class, predominantly white environment quite different from the surrounding lower-income, Latino neighborhood. She was unaware that husbands here found it absolutely unacceptable to allow their wives to be picked up by another man. Most likely, the husbands would have forbidden their wives from coming to the program, or worse, accused them of infidelity. Fortunately, another woman on staff, who had grown up in the community, alerted the director to the plan's pitfall before any damage was done.

· · · · · · · · · · · · · · · · ·

An Anglo elementary school teacher called a conference with the parents of a Native American child who had just joined her class. Much to her surprise, the child's aunt came to the meeting, trailed by several young children. The teacher interpreted the parents' absence as a lack of interest. During the conference, the teacher was further dismayed when the aunt failed to mind her children as they removed books from a classroom shelf. The teacher ended the conference feeling that the student's family was not going to be a strong source of support for his education. The teacher's Native American colleague, however, had quite a different interpretation. Knowing that relatives often serve as primary caretakers in Native American families, she felt that the aunt might have been the most appropriate

As U.S. society grows more diverse, providers, to be effective, must be grounded in the cultures and languages of the families they serve.

Drawing Strength from Diversity

person to attend the conference. Moreover, because the meeting was held in the classroom, she believed the aunt did not correct the children out of respect for the teacher's authority. The aunt would have waited for the teacher to establish the behavioral norms rather than to intrude with her own opinions.

· · · · · · · · · · · · · · · · · ·

An African American social worker became alarmed by the erratic behavior of a Vietnamese teenager who used to attend programs at her youth center. She heard rumors that the youth might be using drugs. She decided to visit the boy's home to discuss the problem with his family. But when she arrived, she could not communicate with the parents because they did not speak English. Noticing his younger sister sitting in the family room, the social worker asked her to translate. The sister agreed, but as the conversation proceeded, the social worker became increasingly suspicious that the sister was not translating the information accurately. At the end of the visit, the social worker took the sister aside. The girl broke down and explained that she couldn't tell her parents what was happening because her brother would beat her up. Meanwhile, the parents felt frustrated because they could not understand what was going on. The incident intensified their fear of losing control over both their children.

· · · · · · · · · · · · · · · · · ·

These real-life vignettes illustrate a dramatic truth: As U.S. society grows more diverse, human services providers and other institutions, in order to be effective, must be grounded in the cultures and languages of the children and families they serve.

Organizations across the country face this challenge. By the middle of the next century, experts predict, the United States as a whole will cease to have a dominant ethnic group. California leads the nation in this demographic shift. Among the state's children and youth, there is already no dominant racial or ethnic group. Collectively, California schoolchildren speak more than 100 languages; one out of three schoolchildren come from a home in which English is not the main language.

In light of this newly emerging society, this report explores strategies for creating the conditions that form the basis of an equitable, multi-ethnic society. Specifically, we focus on the policies and practices of the public and private institutions that provide children, youth and families with health and human services. Ensuring that children, youth and families have access to effective and appropriate supports and services is critical to creating the circumstances that allow people to become educated, successful, contributing members of our nation.

Social worker Cynthia Marshall with children at New Helvetia

Understanding issues of race, culture and language is essential to any effort aimed at improving the current system of supports to children and families.

It is important to bear in mind that our society already suffers from past failures to promote educational and economic opportunities for all racial and ethnic groups. And we are reaping the results of these past failures. During the last twenty years, the poverty rate of young families in the U.S. almost doubled, with racial/ethnic minorities faring the worst. More than 27 million Americans over age 17 are functionally illiterate, with African Americans, Native Americans, and Latinos disproportionately represented. The functionally illiterate cannot read or write well enough to fill out a job application, understand a newspaper, or balance a checkbook. But our nation's history also includes positive, hopeful efforts to serve various racial and cultural groups and to incorporate them into society. This report examines how current initiatives aimed at improving our system of human services can play a critical role in addressing issues of equity and diversity. Our premise is that in a diverse society, negative outcomes can be changed. Grounding the policies and practices of human service providers in an understanding of the culture and language of the families with whom they work is a crucial element.

In the schoolyard shooting case mentioned above, a useful solution evolved only after cultural insight took place. The example of the Latino male driver highlights how lack of understanding could have caused an agency to create problems for its clients and prevent them from using services. The case of the Native American student shows how cultural differences led a teacher to make incorrect assumptions about a family's values. She missed an opportunity to develop rapport with her student's caretaker, a potential ally in the child's education. The last example about the home visit illustrates the importance of agencies being prepared to offer help in a family's native tongue. The absence of any adult who could speak the family's language exacerbated already difficult family dynamics.

This report discusses how understanding issues of diversity — in particular, the implications of race, culture and language — is essential to any effort aimed at improving the current system of supports to children and families. This study builds upon the foundation being laid by current reform efforts, which focus upon interagency collaboration, community decision-making, creative financing, and improved outcomes, among other strategies.

We offer this report as a resource to policymakers, parents, service providers, agency administrators, community activists, evaluators, teachers, consultants, and foundation officers — any of the individuals or groups currently engaged in the hard work of reforming systems that serve children and families, or those who are considering becoming involved in such efforts. Such individuals are the backbone of any reform. Their leadership is critical to ensuring that issues of diversity are addressed. They play key roles in creating the impetus for change and shaping its direction. Many of these colleagues have already played an important role in shaping the content of this publication.

Based upon research conducted in 1993 and supported by the Annie E. Casey Foundation, the Stuart Foundations and the Pacific Mutual Foundation, this report describes information gleaned from site visits to seven collaborative programs; a demographic survey of 98 collaborative programs in California; a literature review; individual interviews; and a retreat to refine our preliminary findings. (See Appendix A for a detailed description of the project methodology). While most of our work focused on initiatives in California, we also drew heavily from the lessons learned from efforts in other states.

This report explores in-depth how issues of race, language, and culture can be incorporated into every stage of the reform process. The following is a brief overview of the report:

Chapter 1: The inextricable links between human services reform efforts and issues of diversity.

Chapter 2: The use of community assessments to engage diverse stakeholders in identifying community strengths and resources; to evaluate the cultural appropriateness of current services; and to define community needs and goals.

Chapter 3: Grounding human services in an understanding of cultural, linguistic and racial diversity: some strategies and approaches.

Chapter 4: Staff development and other steps agencies can take to equip themselves with workers able to respond to the needs of diverse children and families.

Chapter 5: Institutional changes needed to promote culturally and linguistically appropriate services.

Chapter 6: Governance strategies that support inclusive decision-making. (An underlying premise of the report is the need to engage diverse stakeholders in the process of reforming or designing appropriate service and support systems for our nation's diverse families and communities.)

Chapter 7: Recommendations that all groups — ranging from federal and state-level officials to funders and community-based organizations — can take to ensure that issues of diversity are addressed.

Our research demonstrates clearly that addressing diversity requires attention throughout the process — from the techniques a community uses to assess needs and resources to the strategies employed to govern systems and hold them accountable. Creating appropriate services is not just a matter of changing individuals' attitudes and behaviors, but also of re-examining institutional policies and practices.

At the heart of this dialogue are fundamental questions about power: for instance, who has the right to define services for children and families? Creating responsive systems requires changing current power relationships so that agencies and programs can embrace ideas and beliefs other than only those espoused by the dominant culture. An underlying theme throughout this report is the tremendous importance of developing processes that simultaneously foster respect for differences while deepening areas of common ground and understanding.

We view this report as the beginning of an on-going process. It was clear from our research, for example, that no single initiative or person had all the answers. More likely, every community must build its own unique solutions. We hope that this report will stimulate a dialogue that enables individuals, organizations, and communities to begin defining how their programs, policies, and resources need to be reshaped to support the healthy development of all children and families.

CHAPTER 1

Human Services Reform Within a Diverse Society

T his chapter sets the context for discussion of human services reform for ethnically and linguistically diverse communities. It explores the implications of race and culture for institutions that serve families, then examines how current reform efforts are inextricably linked to issues of diversity. The chapter concludes with a discussion on why these reform efforts have not yet focused squarely on diversity. It calls for all readers to begin a much-needed dialogue about how diversity affects all endeavors to improve services and supports for children and families.

Current reform efforts are inextricably linked to issues of diversity.

A. The Implications of Culture and Race

The racial, cultural and linguistic diversity of the United States creates tremendous and complex challenges for institutions that work with families. To understand the roots of this situation, one must recognize that culture heavily affects the approach an agency or individual takes with a client. Culture, in this context, refers to the values, beliefs and traditions of a specific group — the set of rules that guide members' behavior. A group's culture evolves over time. It is influenced by numerous factors, including ethnicity, economic conditions and racial experience. While those of the same cultural group may share similar tendencies, the extent to which any individual abides by those norms is highly variable. It can be affected by many variables, including gender, income, age, sexual orientation, education, and exposure to other cultures.

In the United States, the culture and language of Anglo Europeans have exerted the strongest influences on this country's institutions and social practices. The book, *Developing Cross-Cultural Competence*, by Eleanor W. Lynch and Marci J. Hanson, identifies eight values and assumptions that typify this dominant culture*: 1) the importance of individualism and privacy; 2) a belief in the equality of all individuals; 3) informality in interactions with others; 4) an emphasis on the future, change, and progress; 5) belief in the general goodness of humanity; 6) an emphasis on the importance of time and punctuality; 7) high regard for achievement, action, work and materialism; and 8) pride in being direct and assertive.

. . . .

*Note: The terms "dominant culture," "white," and "Anglo" are often used together or interchangeably (including in this document). Nonetheless, it is important to recognize that they are not the same. In the U.S., the dominant culture is that of Anglo Europeans because of the historical power people of Anglo European descent have held since the founding of the United States. Because this group is racially white, it is often assumed that someone with white skin shares these values. Many whites, however, come from other cultural backgrounds that are not based on the same premises.

Dialogue about cultural and linguistic appropriateness allows for services to reflect the ideas of multiple cultures, not just those espoused by the dominant culture.

Whether providers can articulate them or not, these values often play a significant role in shaping how they respond to a child or family. For example, the emphasis on individualism makes it difficult for a provider to understand decisions made by a person who refuses to act in his own interest because it counters the wishes of his family. The dominant culture also is strongly oriented toward the rational and empirical. Providers who share this orientation have difficulty imagining or devising a response to cultures oriented more toward spiritual or magical belief, such as the Southeast Asian Buddhist community described in the introduction's first vignette. Moreover, because of the historical dominance of Anglo culture, its values and assumptions are typically used to define appropriate behavior and action for all ethnic groups.

Dealing with cultural and linguistic diversity is complex and difficult. Recognizing the extent to which institutions, approaches and actions may be embedded in a culture or language that differs significantly from that of the families being served is only a first step. Once differences are detected, the challenge is to develop an appropriate response. In some situations, the answer is clear. The white teacher in the introduction could gain a better understanding of Native American culture so that she no longer makes inaccurate judgments.

Sometimes, however, a solution is not so obvious. For example, the common U.S. cultural emphasis on achieving individual success through competition and winning clashes with Native American communal values which emphasize tribal achievement over individual glory. Many would argue that the United States would be better off if it embraced some of these alternative values. But figuring out how to respect these communal values in an economic system premised on individual achievement is not easy. For example, a social worker aware of these cultural differences might still have difficulty knowing how to help a Native American man or woman interview effectively for a job. Service providers may also find themselves disagreeing strongly with a value upheld by a family. The U.S. culture, for example, takes a more egalitarian view of women than many other cultures. A teacher who comes in contact with parents whose family traditions cause them to discourage a daughter from continuing her education might be much less inclined to yield to such cultural beliefs.

Nonetheless, the opening vignettes demonstrate the value of engaging people from the community in a dialogue about the cultural and linguistic appropriateness of services provided to them. At a minimum, these discussions are a mechanism for detecting whether a problem exists. Often, they can be instrumental in developing an effective solution. Even when service providers and families do not agree, understanding each other's perspectives can still be a step forward. Such dialogue allows for supports and services to reflect the ideas and values of multiple cultures, not just the ideas espoused by the dominant culture.

The diversity of U.S. society also compels institutions that serve families to deal with race and discrimination. Racial minorities, who are culturally (and often linguistically) different from the dominant ethnic group, continue to confront the challenge of overcoming our country's long history of racial discrimination. Several egregious examples come to mind: Jim Crow laws passed after the Civil War restricted the civil and property rights of African Americans; the genocide of Native Americans and the U.S. government's systematic efforts to deprive them of their land and rights; and exclusion laws that unfairly limited Asian immigration.

While such overt discrimination is now illegal, there is still strong evidence that its legacy continues to plague our institutions. Consider the preliminary findings of the California Assembly's Commission on the Status of African American Males. They found that one-sixth of all black men in California, 16 or older, are arrested each year. Such arrest records haunt these men's job prospects for the rest of their lives. The most troubling finding was that 92% of black men released by the police on drug charges are released for lack of evidence or inadmissible evidence — compared with 64% of whites and 81% of Latinos. The adverse consequences of this situation directly affect the women and children who depend upon these black men for emotional and financial support.

Therefore, developing an effective system of supports calls for exploring how negative outcomes for minority communities might reflect, at least in part, the discriminatory practices of institutions and their employees, whether or not these actions are intentional.

B. The Inextricable Links Between Diversity and Reform

Over the past decade, frustration with the inadequacies of the current system of services for children and families has inspired groups across the country to develop strategies for making services more effective. Operating at local, state and national levels, these reform initiatives typically have involved a broad range of public and private agencies, including schools, social services, probation, health services, community-based organizations (CBOs), and others. Such initiatives have taken a wide variety of forms, among them: linking health and human services with schools; improving school readiness by offering young children and their families a comprehensive array of supports; or moving youth in institutionalized settings (e.g.juvenile hall) to community-based facilities.

These initiatives offer tremendous opportunities to address issues of diversity precisely because they create chances for communities and families to help design and develop services and supports. They also encourage policymakers and providers to reflect upon whether the types of services they wish to provide are appropriate, given the ethnic diversity of families served.

In the past, efforts to reform human services have primarily focused on the need to address the detrimental impact of fragmentation and unnecessary duplication of services. The Institute for Educational Leadership report *Together We Can* summarizes the perceived flaws of the current system. First, services are oriented toward crisis rather than prevention. Second, the current social welfare system divides children and families into rigid and distinct categories (e.g. drug and alcohol abuse, poor academic performance, gang activity, etc.) that fail to reflect interrelated causes and solutions. Third, the current system is unable to meet the needs of children and families due to poor communication among the various public and private agencies that comprise it. Fourth, agencies tend to focus on single issues, hampering their ability to craft comprehensive solutions to complex problems.

However, as the field has gained experience, policy-makers and practitioners have realized that simply changing the relationships among agencies is not enough to fundamentally improve outcomes for children and families. Reformers are now engaging in a broader set of strategies. Emerging experience suggests there are five key elements to reforming systems for children and families[1]:

---

[1] For further information, see *Framework for Systems Reform* produced by the Institute for Educational Leadership.

*Addressing diversity
requires examining
policies and
practices that hurt
particular types
of families or
communities,
then developing
strategies for
change.*

1. Community Decision-making: Systems reform requires the creation of a community governance structure that embraces an inclusive, diverse group of stakeholders from all domains of the service delivery systems and the community. This body's purpose is to guide the reform process and carry out critical policy and leadership functions.

2. Improved Outcomes: Systems reform also requires the definition of specific outcomes — e.g. improvements in the lives of children and families, such as increased educational success or greater family stability— which serve as the underlying goals of a collaborative effort. Such outcomes-based goals facilitate collaboration among agencies and systems because they cannot be achieved by a single entity. They also provide a basis for an on-going system of accountability that holds the collaborating agencies responsible for achieving the stated goals.

3. Effective Services: The services emerging from a reformed system must link public, private and community resources. Services should reflect a new set of principles: community-based; geographically and psychologically accessible; comprehensive and responsive; family-focused and personalized; integrated and culturally and linguistically responsive. Effective services draw upon the informal networks and supports that already exist in communities.

4. Creative Financing: Reforming services involves changing how services are financed so that funding promotes provision of effective services for children and families. Common strategies for changing how services are financed include reallocating existing resources, increasing flexibility in categorical funding streams, and gaining maximum advantage of federal entitlement streams.

5. Leadership Development and Organizational Change: Systems reform requires community leaders to join with knowledgeable, creative and committed public and private agencies in transforming systems and creating organizational models for effective service delivery.

Successfully implementing any of these reforms requires understanding issues of cultural, racial, and linguistic diversity. For example, creating an effective community decision-making structure requires understanding how to reach out to various ethnic and linguistic groups. Furthermore, common understanding must be built among these groups, despite differences in language, racial experience and power status. But many collaboratives find themselves unable to develop strategies to involve key stakeholders from a particular ethnic group because they do not understand the culture or language well enough. Other collaboratives manage to bring all of the stakeholders to a meeting only to discover that the process breaks down, partly because stakeholders are unable to understand each other and define common ground amid cultural and linguistic differences.

Similarly, service providers' awareness of the experiences of racial and linguistic minority groups becomes critical for developing outcomes-based goals that are relevant to all children and families. For example, one collaborative's goals might include strengthening the capacity of families to care for their own children, as well as reducing the number of children placed in "out-of-home care" (foster homes, juvenile hall or institutional care for the mentally ill). One question arises immediately: How does the collaborative define "strengthened families"? Is the goal limited to strengthening the ability of biological parents to care for their young? Or is it more encompassing? In many cultural groups, it is common practice to rely upon grandparents and extended family members to care for youngsters. Will the collaborative's outcome be defined broadly enough so that increasing the number of children living with extended family members is also considered an indicator of success?

Providing coordinated, comprehensive services also requires ensuring that families are not denied access to certain types of assistance because of their race. For example, homeless advocates in one community found that discrimination made it difficult for homeless African American women to move off the streets. When the women went alone to apply for housing, they were often told that a vacancy no longer existed. They were often much more successful if accompanied by a white caseworker. White homeless women, on the other hand, encountered far fewer problems.

Even when service providers understand what type of assistance would be effective for a client from a particular ethnic group, they may not be able to offer such help unless the funding source is willing to pay for it. Advocates working with the African American community have found, for example, that grandparents have had a difficult time being paid to serve as foster parents for their grandchildren, even when it may be in the best interest of the child. The child welfare system licenses only families who are able to provide separate bedrooms for male and female children. But many African Americans (as well as people from other cultures) do not see children of opposite sexes sharing a room as inappropriate. This issue is complicated by economics, since many grandparents also may not have the financial resources to offer children separate rooms.

These examples demonstrate that issues of diversity are inextricably linked to efforts to reform the institutions that serve families. Mutual processes are at work. Reforms will not succeed in improving outcomes for children and families unless they are grounded in an understanding of diversity. At the same time, the reform initiatives are advocating changes that lay a strong foundation for culturally and linguistically appropriate systems of services. Ultimately, a sweeping agenda is needed. Addressing diversity is not just about increasing the understanding and sensitivity of individual providers. It also requires examining whether institutions are engaged (intentionally or not) in policies and practices that hurt particular types of families or communities, then developing strategies for change.

· ·

Note: *This publication focuses on the implications of cultural, linguistic and racial diversity. For many people, however, the term "diversity" encompasses a much broader set of factors, including gender, class, sexual orientation, or physical disability. These factors, which significantly affect how individuals experience the world around them, clearly deserve attention. While we are not able to do justice to all the perspectives that might be encompassed by the term "diversity," this report does make an effort to highlight other issues as they came up in our discussions about cultural, linguistic and ethnic diversity. In particular, our interviews and site visits revealed that concerns about race, language, and culture were often inextricably tied to issues of gender and class.*

C. The Lack Of Attention To Diversity

Although human services reforms clearly offer an opportunity to improve how agencies work with diverse populations, California Tomorrow's five years of studying this area suggest that the issue has not received the attention it deserves. Our work has allowed us the chance to work with a wide range of initiatives (local, state and national) seeking to reform the systems that serve families. While we have been impressed by the tremendous commitment and expertise of the individuals involved in reform, we have also been deeply troubled by the lack of sufficient attention to issues of diversity. In meetings, many participants with the best of intentions discussed coordinating services for children and families without ever questioning whether the services were culturally and linguistically appropriate. If the issue of appropriateness did arise, groups focused solely on simplistic solutions, such as translating materials or holding a single workshop on cultural diversity. Rarely did deeper discusssion surface about whether issues of race, language or culture necessitated changes in program design and policy.

This weakness shows up again in applications for California's Healthy Start initiative, which funds school-linked services efforts that provide health and human services to public school students and their families. Applicants must document the needs of the various ethnic groups being served, as well as detail how they will ensure ethnically and linguistically appropriate programs. Typically, this element of the application lacks thoughtful, in-depth responses.

Poor attention to cultural, racial, and linguistic diversity within the reform movement can be attributed to numerous reasons. First, current reforms tend not to view diversity as central to their work. For example, many efforts commonly focus upon improving communication and coordination among service providers to eliminate duplication of services or improve access for families. Addressing these issues is already an enormous task, and attention to them can override other concerns such as diversity.

Furthermore, many reform-minded groups do not recognize the centrality of diversity because they do not include people who can reflect the perspectives of the diverse communities being served. Yet, engaging such individuals is critical because they bring different resources, knowledge, and skills. They can offer crucial insights into which programs or services would succeed with a particular population and which practices might unwittingly have damaging effects. Interagency collaboration has grown in popularity because service providers see the benefits of using multiple disciplinary lenses to assess a family's needs and strengths and to develop a plan of care that draws upon the resources of multiple agencies. Collaborative processes benefit in similar fashion when they draw upon the insights offered by people of different genders, cultures, racial experiences or economic and class backgrounds. When an effort lacks this diversity, its effectiveness is substantially limited.

Although such lack of diversity within groups sometimes reflects a conscious effort to exclude certain people, it is typically unintentional. Indeed, many groups have come to appreciate the importance of including diverse perspectives. But sometimes, groups may unintentionally exclude others because of the criteria they use to identify who should be included in decision-making processes. Because of historical patterns of discrimination that have led to unequal educational and economic opportunities, people of color often do not hold high-level policy-making positions. As a result, groups may not be diverse if they only invite the usual high-profile players to the meeting. Some groups recognize the need to reach out to particular ethnic groups in their community, but are at a loss because they do not know

While we have been impressed by the commitment and expertise of individuals involved in reform, we have also been troubled by the lack of attention to issues of diversity.

Drawing Strength from Diversity

how to bridge the gaps in culture and language.

Even when reform efforts include people from varied backgrounds and perspectives, this expertise is often not drawn upon. It is challenging to manage a process that involves the participation of linguistically and ethnically diverse individuals. It requires knowing how to build relationships and identify common issues across gaps in culture, language and racial experience. All too often, California Tomorrow observed processes that came to a sudden halt because groups lacked strategies for successfully managing the dynamics of race and power which inevitably arose. Engaging people of varied backgrounds in a conversation about issues of diversity is extremely difficult. One African American man deeply involved in the reform movement explains:

> "It is hard to confront the realities of race without running a substantial risk that someone who is an ally is going to feel attacked or assaulted or feel their integrity has been impugned...Liberals and progressives sometimes feel that they're held to a higher standard on race, that they are the converted, and what we ought to do is go out and preach to someone else...They often can't understand when the issue of race comes up and resolves itself in a relatively angry manner. Then you have a few minorities who are sitting in critical positions who fear having to make a choice as to whether they're going to be pigeonholed into being an advocate of the race or will be allowed to continue whatever other work might have brought them there. The result is neither side realizes there could be constructive engagement around the issue of race."

Often, people avoid discussion because they fear the volatility and pain of raising concerns about equity and diversity. Such discussions extend beyond the professional to the personal realm because everyone comes from a particular racial or cultural background. Consequently, talking about equity and diversity often invokes intensely emotional reactions.

This situation is worsened by the fact that our society has yet to develop effective words to talk about an issue as complex as diversity. Consider the term "racist." This word is commonly used to describe an individual in a position of power who intentionally harms individuals of another racial group through words and actions. This term is also used to characterize a policy or action that has a negative impact on members of a particular racial group, even if it is unintentional. In this case, even individuals with great integrity may be involved unwittingly in a racist situation. Given people's tendency to use the term "racist" loosely without clarifying its meaning, it is no wonder that people often feel their integrity is impugned. This feeling of being attacked and assaulted led a white male involved in the service reform movement to share the following experience:

> "I've participated in a couple of groups where the prevailing technique is to say, 'There are too many white faces around this table. We shouldn't even be talking about the problems at the neighborhood level.' That stance by a person of color just freezes the discussion. Everybody white in the room absolutely drops the subject at that point."

This incident demonstrates how such words by a person of color can silence a potentially useful discussion. They imply that whites in the room have nothing useful to say about the fate of children and families — who in this community are largely ethnic minorities — simply because of their skin color. Yet, as this report describes in more depth later, race alone does not determine whether a person is able to offer effective strategies for supporting children and families. Being of the same race as others in a group does not guarantee that a person will share the same views, beliefs or even culture. Nor does being of a different race indicate that someone has no insight or understanding. Tremendous diversity exists within every racial group and culture, affected by factors such as class and country of origin. Another problem with this approach by a person of color is that it runs the risk of undermining the development of a shared commitment across ethnic groups to ensuring that all children succeed; it contributes to the impression that whites should be interested only in the future of their children.

On the other hand, as mentioned earlier, the above incident also raises a point of concern which California Tomorrow shares — that groups are not inclusive enough. Often, such a reaction occurs because a person of color has become frustrated with situations in which people (typically white) from outside a community constantly make decisions on its behalf without ever consulting the residents. In this case, the challenge is to create a situation where the people who typically make decisions are willing to share their power with others who may not look like them.

The intent of this publication is to encourage much needed dialogue about the implications of diversity for efforts to reform services and supports for children and families. We hope that for some, this document will spark a discussion that has never been able to occur. For others, who have paid more attention to the subject of diversity, we hope this document will help to deepen the dialogue.

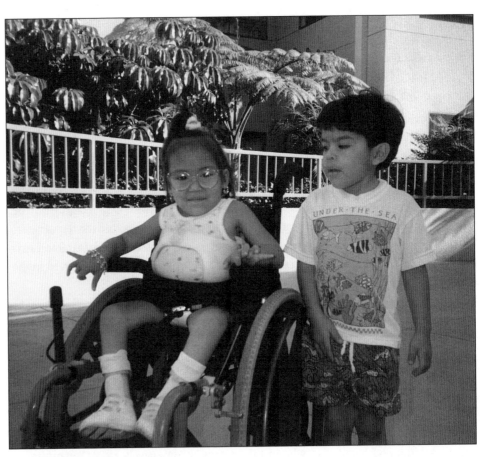

Children Playing at Casa Loma

CHAPTER 2

Community Assessment

Identifying Resources and Needs of Diverse Populations

Typically, community assessments are one of the opening steps in the process of developing new strategies to serve children — and often the first place in which a dialogue about cultural and linguistic diversity can occur. Generally, assessments entail gathering and synthesizing quantitative and qualitative information about the conditions of children and families in a given community, as well as the nature and quantity of existing services and informal supports. Data collection strategies range from reviewing quantitative data already maintained by government agencies to conducting personal interviews, focus groups or community forums, or surveying organizations about their services and available resources. One of the most advanced techniques is data matching, or correlating data across agencies to find out how many agencies may be involved concurrently in serving the same family.[1]

This chapter begins with a brief description of the community assessment process. Then it discusses strategies for using the procedure to involve diverse community stakeholders in identifying community resources and needs, and in determining how the human services system can be reformed to respond to diversity.

A comprehensive assessment can be a process through which diverse community members discover common issues and become invested in working together to benefit children and families.

A. The Promise of Community Assessments

Because of their widespread use, community assessments provide the human services field with an important opportunity for engaging diverse stakeholders in assessing and designing programs. While the nature and depth of such assessments is highly variable, it is clear that community assessments have gained widespread acceptance. Our survey of 98 collaborative efforts found that approximately 85% had conducted some form of assessment as part of the process of developing their programs.

Done well, a comprehensive assessment can be a process through which diverse community members discover common issues and become invested in working together to benefit children and families. Ideally, it is not a one-time event but part of an on-going means of evaluating progress. The assessment becomes a tool for a community to hold itself accountable for achieving the goals and objectives it set out to accomplish; for making adjustments, or knowing when and where to intervene; or for knowing where to target resources.

Assessments are also a chance for the community to "map out" its own strengths and resources and identify potential leaders who can represent the community. Traditionally, human services have used assessments primarily to identify and prioritize the needs of a

---

[1] For more in-depth information about strategies for conducting a community assessment, see *Charting a Course: Assessing a Community's Strengths and Needs,* National Center for Service Integration (Washington D.C.: Fall 1993) and Kretzmann and McKnight, *Building Communities from the Inside Out,* Center for Urban Affairs and Policy Research Neighborhood Innovation Network, Northwestern University (Evanston, IL:1993)

community in order to determine how "outsiders" (e.g. government agencies, foundations, service providers) can most effectively help. In a diverse society where communities deemed in need of service tend to be poor and minority, this deficit-oriented approach can reinforce existing societal attitudes that the communities' residents are less capable and are the cause of their own problems. This orientation toward "needs" and outside intervention as the solution fails to foster the community's internal capacity to intervene on its own behalf. The alternative, which has perhaps been best described in the work of John McKnight, is to use assessments to also map the wide array of community resources and strengths, which could be mobilized to address those same needs.

Assessments are a chance for the community to "map out" its own strengths and resources and identify potential leaders who can represent the community.

Community assessments allow policymakers and practitioners to tap into perspectives essential for designing workable, appropriate solutions. Consider the experience of the Casa Loma affordable housing project, which begins on page 27. In this case, the voices of Latina mothers led to crucial changes in the housing complex design. Their input resulted in locating the child care facility on the second floor to avoid harm from drive-by shootings and redesigning the kitchen so that single mothers could watch their children while cooking.

Conducting a community assessment that leads to effective strategies for supporting children and families requires careful planning by the collaborative. It also requires a willingness to go beyond some of the methods traditionally used in community assessments to ensure that all stakeholders are involved from the outset.

B. Involving the Community in Data Collection and Analysis

Involving individuals who are connected to a community's various sub-groups is key to effective planning, development and implementation of the community assessment process. Such persons can alert the effort to potential political and social taboos and help identify the individuals and organizations with the richest sources of information. They may be able to use their own credibility and information channels to inform the community about the effort and to establish trust. If they live in the community, they are often well-equipped to conduct assessment activities, such as focus groups or interviews. They may be able to identify which locations would put participants most at ease and may also be more aware of how to inspire meaningful conversations.

Involving the community in data collection and analysis is what participatory research is all about. Furthermore, a community assessment process is not just a matter of surveying what people need, but it is a community organizing strategy. By rigorously and creatively assessing community needs, the process gives real "voice" to individuals in the community who have not traditionally been solicited for comment or heard — voices that can significantly influence program design.

Joanna Uribe De Mena, who is involved in a community-wide youth violence prevention initiative in the predominantly Latino Mission District of San Francisco, hopes to put local people to work in conducting neigbhorhood interviews and surveys. She says:

> "The idea is really to get people involved in day-to-day work at all levels of planning and manage it kind of like a political campaign so that if in a year, you come back into the community and talk to people on the street, people will know that this initiative is going on. It won't be just in the domain of community-based organizations or activist parents; they'll have heard about it through posters, contests, radio, television. So that's the vision of how to take a planning process and make it a community activist movement."

It is important to note, however, that living in the community does not mean a person is automatically the best choice for facilitating focus groups or holding interviews. Careful attention must be paid to selecting individuals who can establish the best rapport. In some cases, for example, a community might prefer an "outsider" because it fears an "insider" won't keep the information confidential. On the other hand, some groups would never feel comfortable talking about personal issues with someone from outside the community. Among some groups, factors such as class background, age and gender also can make a tremendous difference. Some people may not feel comfortable talking with an interviewer who is noticeably younger or who is perceived to be of a much higher social class, particularly if that person tends to "talk down" to them. Or women may only feel comfortable sharing certain types of information with another woman.

When the people being served are involved in the data collection and analysis process, their involvement has the potential not only to improve the quality of data collected but also to increase the capacity of community members to analyze conditions surrounding them and to engage in strategies for change.

PROFILE

Everett Middle School:
The Importance of Including Student Voices

 Students from San Francisco's Everett Middle School recently learned valuable lessons about turning their campus into a better place. As part of the California Healthy Start needs assessment and planning process, the youths worked with an outside organization to conduct two separate surveys. The first asked students about their satisfaction with school and what services they would like to see available; the second surveyed local organizations that could contribute resources to Everett.

The initiative, called the Everett Community Bridges Collaborative, was coordinated by St. John's Educational Thresholds Center, a community-based organization in the city's Mission District. St. John's staff was careful to work with a broad array of students, including them in the survey design, data gathering, and analyzing process to foster their leadership skills.

Helping to develop surveys and analyze data gave students a chance to articulate their concerns and contribute positively to the school community. For example, in surveying agencies, students not only asked what services might be available to them but also asked how students could help the agencies. As a result, one local organization that offers interactive educational programs agreed to do workshops for the school. In exchange, several students volunteer at the organization on weekends.

The students also kept busy with the large amount of qualitative and quantitative information generated by the surveys. They analyzed the quantitative data as part of their math course work. Disaggregating the information by ethnicity prompted students to be concerned about how students from all ethnic groups were faring in school.

Then students got creative with the qualitative data by performing a rap song for each classroom so that all students and teachers could hear what the survey had revealed — how students felt about their school, how they wanted to be treated with respect, and how they wanted their confidences honored. Conducting the surveys fostered the ability of kids to understand issues affecting the school community, raised their concerns for their classmates, and made their course work immediately relevant to their life experiences.

Continued on page 20

It takes a deliberate and conscious effort to build the capacity of youth to participate in such a manner. During Healthy Start meetings, St. John's staff member Kyle Fiore sometimes had to prompt shy teens to make constructive suggestions for the program design.

Fiore also has created opportunities for the youth to speak to policy makers. At meetings with the school's student council, the Mayor's Task Force on the Mission, and the San Francisco Board of Supervisors, students have shared their findings and raised the concerns of young people. Students stated overwhelmingly that they wanted to be treated with respect in school and on the street, and that they want to play a proactive, participatory role in their community. Involvement in the assessment planning process also incited the students' interest in community service.

As a result, several initiatives geared toward youth are being implemented at Everett. They include student community service and after-school enrichment projects that place students in volunteer service-provider positions in their school and neighborhoods. These initiatives help to develop students' job readiness and leadership skills. The school has also linked community research projects with classroom curriculum to help motivate students with their academic studies. Everett students have also developed "Student Action Group Rules for Case Managers and Other People," which explains how they wish to be treated and respected by adults.

Such opportunities give youth a strong base not only for exercising leadership but also for developing an awareness that they can indeed have input into issues that affect their lives.

Student Action Group Rules for Case Managers and Other People

We are students at Everett Middle School. We have been meeting every Thursday at lunch to talk about the kinds of services we want and how we think the people who bring us these services should act. We have made a list of rules for people like case managers to follow when they meet with us and other kids:

- ♦ *It can feel weird talking to someone about our problems. Don't rush us to make decisions. We want to go slowly. We don't want to make mistakes.*

- ♦ *Talk to us in a private place.*

- ♦ *Ask us if we want help. Ask us who we want to talk to.*

- ♦ *We want to see the same person all the time.*

- ♦ *We have a right to have our parents with us or whoever we want.*

- ♦ *We want help for our families. Think about our whole families.*

- ♦ *Tell us first before talking to our parents or other adults.*

- ♦ *Bring in people who are all right now and can tell us how they made it through.*

- ♦ *Do what you say you're going to do.*

- ♦ *Give us respect. Look us in the eye. Listen to us properly.*

- ♦ *Don't yell and use bad words.*

- ♦ *Do something nice for our birthday and for the holidays.*

C. The Importance of Disaggregated Data

Particularly when a group is working with limited time or funds, it is tempting to turn to the most readily available information, e.g. data collected and maintained by large public institutions (schools, the health department, the police department, etc.). But such sources often fail to provide a sufficient understanding of what is happening to the diverse groups that make up a community. Such data are frequently available only in the aggregate, rather than broken down by factors, such as racial group, income, linguistic background or gender. Some systems do not collect this information. Others have the information, but are not set up to regularly produce disaggregated reports because they believe such breakdowns are unimportant or too expensive and cumbersome. Also, disaggregated data are often not reported because the numbers are too small to report with any degree of certainty.

Looking at disaggregated data is, however, critical to understanding the conditions facing diverse groups. Aggregate numbers may mask critical and important differences. Consider the results found in Oakland, California, when the Urban Strategies Council, a non-profit research and advocacy organization dedicated to the eradication of persistent poverty, and the Interagency Group for School-Linked Services disaggregated the results of their effort to investigate the extent to which students in eight schools were known to various human service programs.

The aggregate figures demonstrated that two-thirds of all students were known to at least one human service program, and almost a third had used two or more. Thirty percent of the families were found to be using at least one crisis service, such as child welfare or probation. Students performing poorly in school (as indicated by grades, test scores, special education placement, suspensions and absences) were also using crisis services — child welfare, criminal justice and mental health — out of proportion to their numbers.

When the information was broken down further by race and language, distinct patterns emerged. For example, although Asians and African Americans showed very similar use of income maintenance programs, such as Aid to Families with Dependent Children (AFDC), disproportionate numbers of African Americans were known to programs that only intervened in crisis situations, such as homeless assistance, child welfare and juvenile probation. Data from one high school where the enrollment was 86% African American showed that a staggering 42% of African American male students were known to probation. Latino students, on the other hand, were least likely to use any type of service. When data were analyzed by language, it also revealed that limited-English-speaking students used far fewer human services than their English-speaking peers.

Disaggregated data clearly uncovers critical differences between groups. Such findings merit serious discussion among service providers, policy makers, and community members about where to allocate additional services and resources.

D. Drawing Upon Qualitative Data

Interpreting disaggregated quantitative data is a complicated process, however. The previously described disparities might reflect a variety of factors, including income levels, family structure, language, cultural practices and conscious or unconscious discrimination on the part of providers. Gaining a clearer picture of the conditions facing children and families requires a wide variety of data collection strategies — including useful qualitative techniques such as personal interviews, focus groups and community forums — to produce information that adds depth and clarity to the analysis.

Looking at disaggregated data is critical to understanding the conditions facing diverse groups. Aggregate numbers may mask critical and important differences.

*It is extremely
important to hold
focus groups in the
languages spoken
by the community.*

When qualitative strategies are used, language issues become critically important. One of the most well-documented barriers to collaborative efforts is the inability of service providers to communicate with one another because they no longer "speak the same language." Rather, they have become so accustomed to the jargon used by their particular discipline that they no longer employ words and terms understandable to another agency. The potential for miscommunication increases ten-fold when an effort seeks out an even broader array of community residents who may be even less familiar with bureaucratic terms.

Racial and ethnic diversity also increases the potential for miscommunication. Specific words or terms that seem harmless to one person can be explosive or have racist connotations to someone of another ethnic group. Sometimes, because of differences in life experiences, people might ask questions or use words that seem irrelevant to a person who comes from a different background. Many of these issues can be resolved if care is taken before a focus group to test the interview protocols with people from the target community, and then to involve such individuals in design and implementation.

It is also extremely important to hold focus groups in the languages spoken by the various groups in the community. In this country, the norm is to conduct business in the dominant language, English. But even if people can speak some English, they are much more likely to participate in a conversation if they are able to communicate easily and are not worried about whether they are speaking correctly. If more than one language group is represented, it is often important to translate back and forth even though it takes more time. Consider the experience of bilingual project planner Joanna Uribe De Mena, who began one meeting in English and Spanish, but then decided in the interest of time to switch solely to English:

> "To be sure, I asked whether there was anyone in the room who didn't understand English. No one raised their hand, so I proceeded to finish the meeting in English. After the meeting, my colleagues got angry with me. They felt switching to English had in fact limited some people's participation. People who didn't speak English well were not about to admit it in a room full of people."

Another strategy is to divide the group into separate focus subgroups, each conducted in a different language. If focus groups are held separately, it is important to create opportunities for participants to share their ideas across groups. A facilitator or note-taker can translate the information into English for the entire gathering. With the growing diversity in California, collaboratives must also continually build consensus among diverse groups prior to implementing services to avoid dissension later.

E. Creating Incentives for Community Participation in Assessments

One challenge of conducting a thorough assessment is that initially, some people may be uninterested in participating because they do not think any significant policy changes or improvements will result. Communities are all too familiar with assessments required as part of grant applications for foundations or state programs. But an assessment does not guarantee grant funding. And such failure often leaves groups feeling that planning efforts were futile. Even when a grant is received, funding for a program may not become institutionalized. Therefore, services operate so briefly that few concrete benefits are realized. Describing the challenges facing a school-linked service initiative in Oakland, Bruce Marcus, prevention services director at Oakland Community Counseling, offers the following insight:

"There have been a number of initiatives, not just in this community but in other communities, that have been marketed or pitched as, 'This is going to make the difference.' But they didn't make much difference. The challenge is giving parents a reason to hope and trust the process so that they are willing to get involved. But at the same time, we can't build up their hope so high that any result is a disappointment."

One method of attracting community participation in collecting data is to offer a concrete, immediate benefit. For example, some school-linked service efforts have paired a focus group or parent meeting with a family math session where parents learn specific skills to help children with math. Other strategies use stipends or gift certificates to show parents that their time and energy are valued. It helps to consult with parents or community members about appropriate incentives and to ensure that monetary benefits are not considered offensive. Says Claire Brindis of the Center for Reproductive Health Policy Research at the Institute for Health Policy Studies:

"For a lot of people, the consumer's voice has never been heard before. They can be very much taken aback when you come and say, 'How do you feel about this?' Offering incentives can be extremely important. For example, when I did a focus group in one community, we gave parents $15 gift certificates for a local store. Seventeen women signed up to come. All seventeen showed up because $15 meant a great deal to them, and they had never been paid for their time, effort or opinions."

F. Building Trust

Building trust in the assessment process is critical to conducting a successful survey that truly engages a community's diverse perspectives. Many groups, particularly historically oppressed minorities, are highly suspicious of efforts to collect data about their children, families and communities. Such communities have a long history of outsiders who have come to "diagnose" problems and collect data later used to paint negative stereotypes and images of residents' lives and traditions. All too often, such efforts also fail to lead to positive improvements in the community.

Such suspicions are not unmerited, given the negative history of some minority groups with government research efforts. For example, the Tuskegee Syphilis Study involved public health officials who documented for forty years the fate of 399 Black men whose syphilis went untreated. Participants were not educated about the disease or told it was contagious. They were prevented from receiving treatment even though a cure was available and required by state law. The study ended in 1972 only after widespread press attention. The Tuskegee legacy of fear and suspicion continues to haunt subsequent efforts to involve African American communities in planning and researching treatment for newly arising health concerns.[2]

Perhaps a more contemporary problem is families' fears that disclosing confidential or personal information during data collection could put them in jeopardy with the authorities. Particularly during this era of anti-immigrant sentiment, families with members who lack legal immigration status are extremely reluctant to participate because they are afraid of being

Building trust in the assessment process is critical to conducting a successful survey that truly engages a community's diverse perspectives.

---

[2] Myers, Michael, T., "The African-American Experience with HIV Disease," in *Focus: A Guide to Aids Research and Counseling*, Volume 7, No.4, March 1992, p.7.

reported to the Immigration and Naturalization Service (INS). When these suspicions are not addressed, the assessment process not only runs the risk that certain people will refuse to participate, but that some residents might actively oppose the assessment because they believe it counters the best interests of their community.

Given this history, it is essential to build in time and opportunities to describe the assessment to participants and to explain how information will be used. Such background could be presented in various forms throughout the community before the assessment, then provided again as individuals participate in specific components.

G. Beware of Discounting Divergent Perspectives

The problems of distrust are exacerbated when diverse voices raise issues that are discounted

The problems of distrust are exacerbated when diverse voices raise issues that are discounted because they do not fit easily into existing expectations and frameworks. This problem is particularly serious when the voices belong to those who traditionally have not been asked to the table. According to one consultant we interviewed, this happened in one community where she was working:

> "The principal did a wonderful job organizing the advertising focus groups for parents. The staff reached out to Latino parents from a low-income community, as well as Anglo parents from a wealthier, service-rich community. When the parents appeared at the school, they were divided by language group, with the English speakers in one room and the Spanish speakers in another. The English speakers (most of whom were from the wealthier community) responded with, 'We're ready to take over the school.' The Latino parents from the lower-income community said, 'We need help on getting day care,' 'How do I get my kids dental health?' They asked about food. Some didn't have housing. The principal's response to the Latino parents was, 'No, this isn't what we're about. You need to volunteer at our school and work in classrooms.' The school held another meeting, but the Spanish-speaking parents' attendance decreased. The principal, who was Anglo and came from the wealthier English-speaking community, couldn't figure out why."

Obviously, the principal had a different concept of the appropriate relationship between the parents and her school — perhaps because she was white; perhaps because she was English-speaking and didn't understand the language of the parents; or perhaps because she was of a different economic class. Or maybe she was following district orders. Regardless of the reason, her actions further alienated the Latino parents from school participation.

H. Building Understanding of Multiple Perspectives

Clearly, new perspectives must be incorporated to broaden the framework. Some communities have begun to take on this challenge. Maria Casey, executive director of the Urban Strategies Council, recounted the following experience from her work with a consortium of public and private agencies that came together to improve the health of residents in an Oakland neighborhood. The residents, who had been surveyed about their needs, provided revealing answers. Says Casey:

> "Residents prioritized jobs, safety, and cleaning up where they live over purely medical issues...We have to understand that when people are asked about issues that are critical to health and well-being, they tend to define those issues in a quality-

of-life context. Imposing a purely clinical model on this community would not significantly impact broader health issues that beg for holistic responses."

Kathleen Armogida is a former community organizer now employed with the San Diego County Department of Health Services. Her job involves working with the San Diego New Beginnings Collaborative, which offers families a wide range of services, including counseling, transportation and help with welfare, food stamps, and Medicaid eligibility. Armogida shares the following insight:

> "When you engage a community by asking it what it wants and needs, you also have to be prepared to engage in a mutual education process. You can't afford to take the first answer; you have to throw in your 'Yes, buts,' and worry about them with the community. Someplace down the road, you all come to a slightly different understanding of what's real. Then maybe you can talk as colleagues around what it is the community needs. In the meantime, you're doing some other process that tries not to let you be too rigid in your system or your discipline thinking, and on the other hand, manages to sort out from the information you get from the community what is real, authentic, meaningful and relevant. This is real hard work."

Community assessments also provide invaluable opportunities to gain a deeper understanding of how various groups have different views of what is happening within the same community. These insights are crucial to building a more comprehensive picture of the community's assets, strengths, and needs while developing appropriate strategies for improving conditions.

I. Finding Common Ground Across Perspectives

Thorough community assessments are likely to uncover differences of opinion among many different types of groups: between public agencies and community-based organizations; between youth and parents; between ethnic groups; and between families from differing socio-economic levels. An effective assessment process can foster greater understanding and respect for differences, which in turn can help groups identify areas of common ground.

This approach underlies the efforts of the Urban Strategies Council and other Oakland organizations that have embarked upon a youth development initiative. They kicked off with an all-day symposium in which young people, service providers and policy makers who reflected all the ethnicities in Oakland came together to share their perspectives. The experience allowed people to express the concerns of their respective groups. But they also found common ground, in this case, mutual concerns about safety, drugs, and lack of access to quality education. Discovering common concerns among multiple perspectives is more powerful than having someone "dictate" a community's problems. In this way, solutions can be more easily generated from the "bottom-up," rather than from the "top down."

Certainly, in a diverse society, it is easy to find people focusing so much on differences that they lose sight of common ground. One of the most disturbing aspects of our research was how frequently we encountered situations in which lack of understanding and communication bred animosity between groups. For example, low-income whites and blacks would blame their impoverished economic conditions on Asians or other newly arrived immigrants. They often saw the growth of Asian-run businesses as a sign that Asians were getting "special" help from the government. The people making these comments were unaware that

An effective assessment process can foster greater understanding and respect for differences.

Asian communities often use a traditional, informal system of credit to create capital investments, even in areas where banks are unlikely to offer loans. In at least one site, these types of animosities were creating a political problem for the human services reform efforts, which were seen as yet another attempt to help one group at the expense of another. A very different scenario might have emerged if the groups involved were given opportunities to better understand their respective situations and to discuss how they might work together to improve the overall economic conditions of their neighborhood. Says Maria Casey of the Urban Strategies Council:

> "I have found a willingness in Oakland for people who are culturally diverse to come to the table and be very candid about what they feel ought to happen. They are quite vocal about what is not going well for the populations they represent, but exhibit a real willingness to begin to work through tough issues. These often fragile relationships are truly tested when funding or development resources mandate the prioritization of one group or one area over another. However, we have found that making...information accessible about...strategies that can make a difference across ethnic lines can help to mediate conflict. Working through issues of diversity requires that we understand that we're not all the same, but that we do have some of the same issues."

J. Conclusion

Ultimately, the assessment process offers a valuable tool for bringing a community together to begin developing corporately agreed-upon outcomes for children and families. As the later chapter on institutional change will discuss, these community-defined goals and objectives can also be used to hold agencies and service-delivery systems accountable.

CHECKLIST FOR PRACTITIONERS

Conducting a Community Assessment

- ♦ *Engage diverse stakeholders in conducting the community assessment and in collecting and analyzing the data.*
- ♦ *Look at ethnic-specific data to understand how well institutions are currently serving various populations.*
- ♦ *Draw upon qualitative as well as quantitative data.*
- ♦ *Create incentives for community participation in assessments.*
- ♦ *Allow for time and opportunities to build trust within the community.*
- ♦ *Use the assessment process as an opportunity to identify strengths and resources of various ethnic groups residing in the community.*
- ♦ *Use the assessment to gain insight into the perceptions of various groups that make up a community.*
- ♦ *Use the community assessment process to identify areas of common ground across diverse perspectives.*
- ♦ *Use common ground to develop desired outcomes for children and families across ethnic groups residing in the community.*

PROFILE
Casa Loma

 Anna Rodriguez was looking for a better life for herself and her four sons when she heard from a friend about Casa Loma, a new, 110-unit housing development located on a small hill just west of downtown Los Angeles. Affordable rent was an issue for Rodriguez, a single parent, but she wanted to live in a nice-looking building. Child care, security, a safe place for her kids to play, and a sense of community also mattered. Rodriguez happened to see an advertisement announcing Casa Loma's focus on single heads of households. The ad touted the very same things for which she was searching. She submitted her name, along with 2,300 other applicants, and won a unit through the lottery that was held.

Rodriguez says she and her family wouldn't have the kind of life that they have now if they were not living at Casa Loma. In fact, she and other residents even participated in the housing design and helped determine the types of support services Casa Loma offers, ranging from child care and family counseling to literacy and English classes.

Moving Toward Self-Sufficiency

Including residents in decisions that affect their lives fits into Casa Loma's philosophy of developing self-sufficiency. The unusual housing development, which targets low-income families, senior citizens, and single parents, takes a hands-on approach to helping families improve their lifestyles. Or, as Casa Loma Director Sandra Villalobos said, "To help families achieve the goals they are looking for." Ulti-

Anna Rodriguez and family

mately, Casa Loma hopes to build the local community's capacity to become self-sufficient.

Casa Loma is located in the Belmont area of Los Angeles' Pico Union District, where Central Americans make up about 60% of the population. During the last decade, the neighborhood surrounding Casa Loma has become home to newly arrived immigrants not just from Central America, but from Mexico and various Southeast Asian countries as well. Many people labor as garment workers, janitors, street vendors, or restaurant employees, earning $30 a day and living in poverty. The residents of Casa Loma reflect the neighborhood population. Many are recent immigrants, speak very little or no English, or head single-parent households.

For these residents, the linking of affordable housing to support services are "the catalyst to empowering families" by increasing their ability to provide for themselves, said Maggie Cervantes, the executive director of New Economics for Women (NEW), the economic development corporation that created Casa Loma.

Continued on page 28

Many Casa Loma residents were attorneys, doctors, and nurses in their home countries. In the U.S., they hope to become medical assistants or nurse aides. A Casa Loma social worker helps them to work toward dreams and goals. According to Villalobos, NEW wants to demonstrate "that immigrant families are motivated, can work and will work, and that they don't like living under impoverished conditions...It's not their fault. Barriers exist, and immigrants are hard-working people just like the rest of us."

"The motivation of immigrants is to have their own home and business," added NEW Board Chair Bea Stotzer. "The issue is not isolation. They want to succeed. It's not an issue of dependency, but hunger for knowledge. The integral part of our vision is to be able to give them the skills to think, and have the self-esteem to go out and succeed on their own wherever they are."

Anna Rodriguez was among the community mothers given the chance to help determine Casa Loma's housing specifications and types of services offered. For example, proposed walk-in closets were redesigned because the women said that extended family members would want to come live with them by turning the closets into bedrooms. To cope with the challenge of cooking meals while watching over their children, the mothers asked for the apartment to have a social area connected to the kitchen. The original plan called for separate kitchen and dining areas.

Residents Determine Services

To improve service delivery to residents, Casa Loma entered into strategic partnerships and collaboration with nearby, community-based organizations and agencies, such as the Los Angeles Unified School District, the Boys and Girls Club, Centro Latino Educación Popular, Centro de Niños, and the Central Library.

Residents of all ages benefit from an array of on-site services and programs, all determined by community input, including: child care; individual and family counseling; literacy and ESL classes; parenting classes; and other educational and recreational activities. Casa Loma used its redevelopment fees to hire a social worker to meet with families. Residents favored this route, which they believed would bring them someone more responsive culturally and linguistically, rather than to seek the assistance of a public agency.

With support from the Mattel Foundation, plans are underway to create an inter-generational learning center and computer lab modeled after programs at the nearby PUENTE Learning Center. In addition, the National Association of Latino Elected and Appointed Officials (NALEO) plans to sponsor a citizenship drive.

Casa Loma's Beginnings

Casa Loma's development was borne out of the observations of a group of women from a national Latina organization, Comisión Feminil. The women were concerned that public policy discussions about poverty did not reflect women's perspectives. In 1983 Comisión formed a task force of five women to review the economic issues facing Latinas. The task force studied the impact of the Reagan Administration's social services cuts on the community and found fewer support mechanisms available for women and families. They also uncovered a great need for affordable housing.

"The group redefined the approach to addressing poverty," said Stotzer, who was a task force member. "Traditionally, the approach ignores the burden of Latina women. It misses how Latinas value family. There is also little understanding of how economic conditions force families to move from one neighborhood to another, from one economic class to another."

About the same time, Stotzer read an article by a female architect in MS Magazine. The story presented an overview of service integration at housing developments during World War II for women who had to go to work to replace the men who went off to war. The article helped shed light on the kind of project that the task force wished to embark upon. Comisión Feminil formed NEW as a separate economic development corporation to deal with women and poverty issues and to embark on an affordable housing development that included child care.

According to Stotzer, NEW was particularly concerned about designing Casa Loma and its services from the perspective of the Latina community:

> "In these families, women are the ones who generally control the purse strings. The mother makes the decisions of the household. She decides what the atmosphere of the home is, the kind of education the children receive, the place of residence, and is responsible for self-esteem and the development of her children. Men see things from a different paradigm. Therefore, a woman's input (in service design and delivery) is paramount. Otherwise, services wouldn't be designed appropriately to really benefit the customers we are serving."

In discussing services, issues of diversity surfaced quickly. When NEW started on the Casa Loma project in 1987, the majority of the surrounding community was Mexican American. In 1993 there is a mix of Mexican American and Central American populations. It was clear that Central Americans would need different kinds of counseling services. In addition, different parenting education issues came up because this group was more recently arrived than NEW initially thought. The program had to design a way to teach parents how to use U.S. institutions, such as schools and food stamps. The program also helped orient newcomers to U.S. culture. For example, some Central American women, accustomed to having to bribe people for help back in their homelands, had to be instructed that the practice was frowned upon here.

Not only was the Central American population growing, but so was the Korean community. Public service announcements and newspaper notices advertising Casa Loma were run in Spanish and Korean. Hence, the lottery resulted in a much more diverse mix of families than originally expected, intergenerationally as well as multiculturally. A number of Korean families won units through the lottery, as did many seniors who indicated that they didn't want to be segregated from children and families, but wanted to be included in everyday activities.

Upon moving into their units in the summer of 1993, every family was given an explanation of the purpose of Casa Loma and of their obligations. Some families decided against taking up residence because of these guidelines. Casa Loma officials recognize that different strategies are required to serve and to communicate with the various groups. Officials have translated the resident council booklet into different languages and have made an effort to learn particular customs, for example, taking off one's shoes when entering a Korean home.

Eventually a Korean staff assistant and translator who can work more efficiently with Korean families will be hired. In the meantime, Director Villalobos feels she has the care and patience to communicate with Korean parents through various means. She said she tries to be as culturally sensitive as possible and always tells people, "Please, if I offend you, let me know. Or, you teach me, and I'll teach you." And somehow, people do always let her know what they need or want. For example, Korean families said they wanted water filters, so Casa Loma installed the devices.

Continued on page 30

Finding Committed Board Leadership

To date, the majority of NEW's Board of Directors have been women. Stotzer had set out to pull together a board with the right clout. She wanted people she trusted and whose first priority was the community. She also found a Latina attorney knowledgeable about affordable housing and financing. "Women face intractable discrimination when it comes to financial help and board room politics," Stotzer said. "It is presumed that women have no knowledge or expertise in these arenas. We decided to combat that discrimination by creating affordable housing and programs to support that housing which helps raise women from poverty wages to livable wages."

The Board also has male representation because Stotzer (who eventually became the Board Chair) wanted to have a male perspective when negotiating a deal. The Board agreed upon the following principles for working on this project: that the Board would control the development; that the project increase the capacity of Latinas for economic development; and that the site would provide child care space.

Two focus groups were conducted early in the development and planning stages of Casa Loma. A 50/50 mix of Central American and Mexican immigrant families participated. Child care, safety, and learning English were the top concerns of community mothers. Stotzer feels that these issues would not have been raised if the focus groups had not been held. Stotzer, like most of the other women involved with NEW, is Latina and grew up in a relatively poor family. While the insights gained from having this background helps the Board and the staff to make appropriate program design issues, it is not always sufficient. For instance, when the project was first conceptualized, NEW thought it might be preferable to construct townhouses instead of a single apartment building. But the community mothers involved in the design questions felt such a plan would not offer them the safety or community feeling they desired.

The Casa Loma experience has also shown that reaching out to a community requires perceptiveness and attention. For example, NEW found that it needed to keep the architect away from discussions with the women about building design. An architect in the room would have caused the women to remain silent because they would have deferred to his expertise. NEW also took special care to hire a Spanish-speaking facilitator who had the skills and experience to make the mothers feel at ease. They found Villalobos, who has since become the Casa Loma director. A single teen mother herself, Villalobos had worked in clinics with Central Americans and Mexicans. At Casa Loma, her interaction with residents is constant. She knows everyone: their names, where they live, how many children they have.

An Approach for Community Economic Development

Ultimately, NEW's goal is not just to increase self-sufficiency of families, but also to work on community economic development: to enhance the capacity of people to become community and business leaders. Realizing that NEW needed its own committed people on the development team, the Board encouraged a number of its own members to step down, start their own businesses, and join the development team, which already consisted of an experienced construction contractor, engineer, and design consultant for the child care space.

Residents Take on Ownership

Casa Loma has experienced rapid success in seeing leadership develop in other areas as well. NEW Board members thought it would take six months for families to move in and settle before organizing. But after only three weeks, they took the initiative to organize their own residence council, with Latino, Korean, and African American representatives. Currently, the council mainly organizes social activities, such as community "comida tipica" potlucks, but it also participates in resolving most of the "small" issues that arise, such as rumor control.

Casa Loma's young people are also taking on ownership. A youth "Torch Club," organized by Youth Director Eric Solis, aims to teach about our democratic heritage, in part by taking youths out to do community service. In planning a neighborhood clean-up, the kids even went to their city councilman to ask for paint brushes. The 11- to 13-year old members have organized themselves into hall monitors. They watch out for the safety of younger kids, make sure they do not run in the hallways, and keep the hallways clear of trash. The youths feel a new a sense of power and control of their lives and are taking on leadership roles, Solis said. They have elected their own club president, vice president, treasurer and recorder.

A cultural issue has presented itself, however, one that symbolizes the changing relationships between teen-agers and their parents. Kids becoming independent have expressed a desire to meet with their parents to talk about leaving them alone — that they are able to take care of themselves. But Villalobos, attuned to her responsibility to all residents and to her need for continued trust with parents, told the youths to hold off. The parents, who expect respect from their children, may not yet be prepared for such a dialogue, she said.

Casa Loma's Future

What lies in the futures of Casa Loma residents? NEW Executive Director Maggie Cervantes said, "The next step for many of these families is starting their own business and moving to a better neighborhood; to get involved in community organizing to improve their neighborhood."

In fact, one week before the Los Angeles riots broke out, Casa Loma had an arson fire. More than 1,000 flyers were sent out asking the community for help in identifying the arsonists. The flyers explained that the culprits were destroying housing for children and families. During the riots, there were neighborhood people "watching out" for Casa Loma. Casa Loma is now the "watchdog" for the neighborhood, said Stotzer.

One of the ways NEW gauges how well it continues to do its job is to have Casa Loma's social worker and family counselor Emily Catho visit with families every two months to assess their goals, such as purchasing a business, learning English, or buying a home. Soon, Catho will provide a report to Cervantes on the overall needs of families. Keeping its social worker once redevelopment fees are depleted presents an issue Casa Loma will have to face down the road.

For now, resident Anna Rodriguez is happy to be at Casa Loma. She has time to study English and doesn't worry about her children while she is at work. Rodriguez wants to study fashion design and hopes to open her own business eventually. "Life is easier now that I am living here at Casa Loma," she said. "It's always changing for the better."

CHAPTER 3

New Strategies for Working with Diverse Children and Families

C ommunity assessments are only a beginning step toward better services for diverse children and families. Once an assessment has been completed, the question remains: How will agencies and service providers respond successfully to the information gleaned?

One response would involve grounding services in an understanding of cultural, linguistic and racial diversity, which could improve their effectiveness. This chapter focuses on strategies for doing so because boosting effectiveness of services is a key goal among efforts to change systems. Embedded in this discussion are issues of professional practice, as well as program design.

This chapter begins with a discussion of innovative reforms already being employed to improve services, including:

♦ focusing on families, not just individual members

♦ emphasizing interdisciplinary collaboration

♦ being consumer-driven

♦ promoting self-sufficiency

♦ adopting an "assets" orientation toward clients and communities, instead of a "deficit" one

One of the exciting findings of this report is that each of these strategies already opens the door for (and arguably requires) service providers to pay greater attention to issues of diversity. While these new approaches are important first measures, they may not be sufficient alone to create systems fully responsive to diverse populations. As the last part of this chapter discusses, fully grounding efforts in an understanding of diversity involves giving people (service providers and clients alike) the opportunities to deepen their understanding and appreciation of their own identity and to increase their comfort and skills in multicultural settings.

A. Family-Focused Services Can Increase Respect for Culture and Language

A major criticism of the current system of service delivery is that most programs for children and families focus only on the issues facing one member without exploring how they may be related to the issues of other members. In reality, what happens to one family member inevitably affects the rest. A child's life cannot be separated from the fate of his or her family. Recognition of this problem has led a growing number of practitioners, policymakers and advocates to promote services that support the well-being of the entire family.

In a diverse society, figuring out which family members to enlist requires knowledge of cultural background because family structure often differs among ethnic groups.

Adopting a family-focused approach means embracing all members. For example, rather than just offering tutorial services to elementary school children, a program would provide a comprehensive array of additional services for other family members, such as job employment and training activities or GED classes. Or some programs (such as those that promote the literacy of children and their parents) would offer services that can be used by different family members simultaneously.

Family-focused approaches also recognize the critical importance of involving other family members in efforts to serve children. In a diverse society, however, figuring out which family members to enlist requires knowledge of cultural background because family structure often differs among ethnic groups. In many families, particularly in those that stress the roles of extended family members, it would be a mistake to assume that parents are a child's primary caretakers or that parents can make decisions about a child's future without the approval of other relatives, such as the child's grandparents.

Supporting families also requires understanding the critical roles that culture and language play in the health and well-being of families. A family-focused perspective can help alert service providers to situations in which they might not be paying enough attention to the language or the culture of a family. Consider

Vietnamese children in Denver, CO

the development of the "Torch Club" described in the Casa Loma profile in Chapter 2. Designed to teach youth about democratic principles, the Torch Club helped young people gain a greater sense of power and control in their lives. But when the youths expressed a desire to meet with their parents to ask for greater independence, the director realized that she had overlooked an important component of the program. For parents who expect children to respect their authority, this type of behavior would violate their cultural norms. The director had neglected to simultaneously work with parents so that they could understand and respond to the transformations within their children.

Language issues are equally important. Researchers, for example, are beginning to find that early care and education programs that emphasize English without paying adequate attention to the home language may be creating situations in which children learn English at the expense of their home language. Programs that do not use a child's home language reinforce existing societal messages that it has a lower status. Keenly aware of status differences, children from language-minority families will often refuse to speak that tongue, thereby ceasing to develop their primary language skills.

The loss of the primary language is a tragedy for a number of reasons. First, language is a main vehicle for transmitting culture. Many words and concepts do not translate easily from one language to another. Language is a critical source of a child's sense of identity and cultural heritage.

Second, if language loss occurs and the parents do not speak English, the effects on family functioning can be even more disastrous. Unlike their children, language-minority parents are much less likely to have opportunities to learn English. Many work several jobs just to survive and have no time to take English as a Second Language courses, which often have long waiting lists anyway. Many are relegated to unskilled, low-paying jobs that do not require them to speak English.

Children who only speak English cease to share a common language with their parents. Parents are in a sense "robbed" of their ability to raise their children in the fullest sense — to pass on their values, advice, and knowledge, or even to help with homework. Awareness of these issues helps providers to understand the importance of encouraging children to maintain their home languages and of helping parents to gain opportunities to learn English.

B. Inter-disciplinary Collaboration Can Foster Cross-Cultural Understanding

Service providers from ethnically different backgrounds can benefit from colleagues' knowledge about different cultures.

The need to take a more holistic approach to working with children and families has led virtually all current reform efforts to emphasize collaboration among different types of service providers. Such collaboration allows service providers to move beyond a narrow disciplinary perspective by drawing upon other colleagues' skills, resources and abilities. Collaboration also encourages providers who may be working with different members of a family to labor together and share insights.

For example, Yoland Trevino, the director of a school-linked service center, finds that a major part of her role involves sharing her expertise about services with educators. In return, the educators advise Trevino about the academic issues facing children who take part in center activities. Trevino says:

"Educational institutions do not promote a holistic approach to teaching that embraces the family and the environment. Because we've had involvement with the family, I have a somewhat greater understanding of the larger picture....I use staff in-services, retreats and personal contact to raise teachers' awareness of the multi-stresses facing their students. So many educators have false notions and perceptions of how things ought to be. As a result, they may label or judge children without a full understanding of the real circumstances."

An environment that encourages staff to share their various disciplinary perspectives can also enable service providers from ethnically different backgrounds to benefit from colleagues' knowledge about different cultures. Barbara Carr, an African American family worker and case manager from the Family Mosaic project, a collaboration of mental health agencies in San Francisco, says:

"What has helped me is working with a team of people which includes a mix of ethnic as well as disciplinary backgrounds. Working in this agency has allowed me the freedom to turn to fellow co-workers and ask questions about various aspects of other cultures."

Carr's co-worker Eileen Mendez explains,

"Based on our own experiences, we all come with preconceived notions about how we expect people to behave. We can put our foot in our mouths by saying a question or a comment in the wrong way. What is helpful about this particular agency is that we're all trying to get along together. Issues of race are still difficult to talk about, but they are raised and discussed because Family Mosaic staff want to dispel myths about themselves."

Cultural misunderstandings are a natural occurrence when people work in cross-cultural situations. But, Mendez's last comment also suggests, the work environment plays a critical role in determining whether workers feel comfortable sharing their knowledge of racial and cultural issues with their colleagues. Talking about issues of race and culture is not always easy. Family Mosaic's safe climate stems from acknowledging that everyone makes mistakes and that dialogue helps address biases. (See page 69 in Chapter 5 for additional strategies for encouraging dialogue among diverse staff.)

Interracial teaming can also increase the effectiveness of services by enabling people from different ethnic backgrounds to build upon each other's skills and credibility. This is exactly what occurred in Denver, Colorado, when a white Child Protective Services (CPS) worker was outstationed at one of the Family Resource Schools that serves many Spanish-speaking families. (Family Resource Schools emphasize parent empowerment and education strategies to help parents become more involved with their children's education. For further information, see page 83.)

School staff wanted the CPS worker to help families understand the resources available through social services and how to avoid becoming involved with the Child Protective Services system. The staff was also painfully aware, however, that many of the families already viewed CPS workers with suspicion because of negative experiences with the child welfare system. The fact that the worker was white and spoke no Spanish did not help the situation.

Consequently, as soon as the social worker stepped foot on the school, she was teamed with the family resource coordinator, a Spanish-speaking Latina who had already gained the trust of the community and the Latina school principal. In addition to serving as a translator, the coordinator used her presence to pass along to the CPS worker the trust she had already built with families. The principal and the coordinator introduced her at as many school events as possible as someone who had come to help them. Over time, the CPS worker not only gained the confidence of the families, but also her experience at the school led her to become a strong advocate for bilingual services within her own agency.

C. Client/Family-Centered Approaches Can Improve Cultural Appropriateness

Increasingly, reform activists are recognizing that services are most effective when clients are included in the collaboration. This shift to a client-centered or "consumer-driven" approach views families as a critical source of information about what types of assistance would be most useful. It also acknowledges the simple fact that people are more likely to benefit from a service if it is something that they feel they want and need.

While a client-centered approach is not explicitly about diversity, it can increase the chances that providers will offer culturally appropriate assistance. Service providers can find ways to help families based upon the values and the beliefs of the families, even if they differ from those that the service providers espouse by virtue of their own background or professional training. Abner J. Boles III, PhD., director of the Family Mosaic Project and director of child and youth health services of the Department of Public Health, explains:

> "People come with their own biases, reflecting their personal experiences, agency perspectives, professional training. We try to break down the racist aspects of that background by telling staff to start from scratch. Take the time to ask a family about their culture, their needs, their expectations, and discuss which strategies have worked or not worked for them. Then we give workers the flexibility to design services based on this information. Services offered this way are more likely to be culturally appropriate."

Service providers can find ways to help families based upon the values and the beliefs of the families, even if they differ from those that the service providers espouse.

Taking a client-centered approach is, however, not always easy, particularly when the service provider and the family are from different cultural backgrounds. It is easy to misunderstand each other's actions or words. When working in such situations, providers need to be skilled in cross-cultural communication. In some cultures, for instance, silence means consensus. In others, silence is a polite way of indicating disagreement. Providers need to be aware of these differences and how to navigate around them.

Moreover, a client-centered approach works only if family members are able to express their opinions and wishes to the provider. Often, however, family members feel they are in no position to do so. Because the provider determines whether the client should receive a particular resource, these relationships are typically unequal — a situation exacerbated if racial, gender and class differences exist. Consider, for example, if a provider is white and a recipient, African American. This situation replicates historical patterns of inequality. The service provider needs to understand the implications of these dynamics and how to build trust despite them.

Another challenge worth further exploration is how service providers should handle situations in which their views are at odds with a family's. How should a provider weigh the knowledge gained from professional experience and training against the very real need to respect the wishes of the family? While this type of situation can arise with any family, it is even more likely in cross-cultural situations.

D. Emphasizing Self-Sufficiency Can Promote Greater Attention to Equity

Many policymakers and practitioners have come to the conclusion that services must increase the self-sufficiency of clients rather than perpetuate dependency. In recent years, support for this emphasis has come from a wide range of conservative and liberal perspectives. James Johnson, an African American outstationed social worker at the Del Paso Heights project in Sacramento, says:

> "Most people are in the system for a reason — not because they want to be — drugs, lack of education, etc. We find out what their needs are and help them get the support to make them independent. It is one stop-shopping; we have employment, eligibility, food assistance...We view ourselves as resources, connecting tools within agencies and within communities. It's not just giving the client a phone number but making arrangements, introducing the client, following up. We aren't just another agency that gives services that perpetuate the system. The goal is to give them tools so they don't need us."

This focus on self-sufficiency can come in numerous forms. Sometimes it means that a program will stress activities, such as developing literacy or job interviewing skills or teaching English as a Second Language, so that family members can eventually find jobs and support themselves. At other times, it means changing the incentives of the current system so that work pays. It involves, for instance, ensuring that mothers formerly on welfare have access to child care assistance and health care so that they are less prone to returning to public assistance.

However, the effectiveness of these strategies depends upon economic opportunity. Job training, for instance, only succeeds when jobs are available. To have long-term impact, a focus on self-sufficiency must be combined with willingness to address historical patterns of discrimination and inequity that deny many residents of poor and minority communities

To have long-term impact, a focus on self-sufficiency must be combined with willingness to address historical patterns of discrimination and inequity.

access to resources that would allow them to be self-sufficient. The Consumer's Union report *The Thin Red Line: How the Poor Still Pay More* documents vividly how low-income communities continue to confront redlining by banks and commercial institutions, a situation that deprives poorer areas of basic services, such as access to reasonably priced grocery stores and financial services available to more affluent neighborhoods.

It is not surprising that during community assessments, jobs and housing are among the most frequently cited "needs". A promising trend among the many reform efforts is an increased emphasis on community economic development and building the capacity for self-sufficiency.

E. Assets-Orientation: A Way to Build Upon the Strengths of Diverse Families and Communities

Increasing individual and community capacity for self-sufficiency is closely related to the growing belief in focusing upon assets rather than deficiencies. In today's system, most programs use deficiencies to decide whether and how services are provided. People obtain services by demonstrating they are somehow flawed: they are sick, failing school, addicted to drugs, etc.

This "deficit orientation" occurs at the individual and community level. Providers often begin working with a family by conducting a family needs assessment, which helps determine the family's eligibility for various services, as well as the types of assistance the family desires. Similarly, on the community level, programs are often required to conduct needs assessments to justify whether proposed services are appropriate and necessary.

The problem with this approach is that people and communities soon come to be defined primarily by their deficiencies. But "needs" are only a part of the picture. Each family or community also has assets and resources that often go unrecognized. In their book *Building Communities from the Inside Out: A Path Toward Finding and Mobilizing A Community's Assets*, John Kretzmann and John McKnight explain that deficit-oriented policies and programs create situations in which:

> "[People] begin to see themselves as people with special needs that can only be met by outsiders...They think of themselves and their neighbors as fundamentally deficient, victims incapable of taking charge of their lives and of their community's future."

In contrast, a strengths-based approach to delivering services places at least equal if not greater emphasis on helping individuals and communities to recognize and develop their own capabilities.

While this shift is positive under any circumstance, it is particularly important in a diverse society. Typically, the criteria used to define who "qualifies" as a problem is set by those in power, i.e. members of the dominant cultural group. Those communities and individuals who are culturally different from the dominant group are most likely to be considered a problem. As a result, they bear the greatest impact of the deficit approach.

A strengths-based approach can occur in several ways. At a minimum, a provider can begin probing families' strengths and assets in addition to asking about their needs. Yoland Trevino directs Los Angeles' Vaughn Street Family Center, which provides comprehensive health, educational and social services to students and their families. She explains:

"My role is more as a nurturer and facilitator for helping families identify their own strengths and build on those strengths. My goal is to help families discover their own voice and a sense of their own power."

This approach also can be reinforced through program design. The Vaughn Family Center, for example, helps families find their own strengths through a service exchange bank. Whenever a family seeks assistance, it must identify a "service" that it will offer in return—anything ranging from babysitting for a school activity to tutoring a child or helping another parent. That way, parents are not only receivers, but givers.

A program also can have a highly positive impact when it is purposely designed to validate the strengths of the diverse communities it serves. Most commonly, programs can affirm the positive attributes of a community by creating a warm, friendly office environment that welcomes clients through art work, pictures, and multilingual signs. Paying attention to such details is important. What people see when they walk into a room often sets the tone for future interactions.

A program also can have a highly positive impact when it is designed to validate the strengths of the diverse communities it serves.

Environment is only one step, however. The strengths-based approach has prompted many to advocate another key strategy for improving services: helping communities to sustain and develop their networks of informal supports. Such supports range from neighborhood groups to the strong, extended networks of friends and relatives that many members of ethnic groups can rely upon for financial support during crises.

Sometimes, informal supports exist because public-spirited individuals who live in a community spend their personal resources and energies on activities, such as providing hot meals to youngsters or organizing neighborhood watch programs.

In a diverse society, however, the nature of informal supports can vary widely. Practitioners must be skilled in discovering the assets within different ethnic communities. Art Bolton, director of the Center for Integrated Services for Families and Neighborhoods and a chief architect in the effort to create a community-based, integrated service program in Sacramento's Del Paso Heights, explains:

"What are the strengths of an African American, Hispanic, or Asian community group? What can we build upon that could lead to good outcomes? In Del Paso Heights...we are trying to develop a neighborhood garden. A principal at a neighborhood school informed us that Asian families living in the neighborhood asked to use some of the land at the school to build a community garden. Living in apartment houses, they don't have a place to grow their vegetables. So we plan to tap into the Asian community for consultation and expertise. Similarly, in the black community, one of the strengths is and has been for generations, the strength that comes out of the black church. People are already organized; they have a common place to go and they share a religion, but it's more than a religion. There are cultural activities in that church. So how do we support that? How do we nurture it?"

F. Additional Strategies

For California and for the nation, diversity is perhaps our greatest asset. We can only benefit from this asset, however, if people are able to value differences while recognizing common goals and interests. How services are delivered can play an integral role in helping people develop this ability.

California Tomorrow's work suggests that promoting this ability requires a multi-faceted approach: supporting the efforts of ethnic groups to establish a strong sense of identity and group solidarity, and at the same time, creating opportunities for diverse peoples to learn about each other, identify common ground, and build ability to operate in multicultural settings.

Too often, efforts to strengthen group consciousness are viewed as the polar opposite of initiatives to foster understanding among groups in an integrated setting. In contrast, our work suggests that both approaches are interrelated aspects of the same effort.

1. Building an Internal Sense of Identity and Group Consciousness

Spending time among members of one's own ethnic group is an important developmental experience, potentially a key step toward realizing one's strength and power. When individuals who have confronted racism or prejudice lack opportunity to understand that others in their group have suffered the same experiences, it is easy to blame the problem on personal deficiencies rather than on larger social and political issues.

Being with one's own ethnic group also gives people a chance to better understand their culture and traditions, as well as provide important insights into why they behave in certain ways. Ethnic-specific activities can be critical to developing the conditions under which groups can successfully work together in integrated settings.

Consider the experience at the Vaughn Family Center. Located inside a Los Angeles elementary school, the collaborative provides comprehensive services to the campus' pupils and their families. (The center and school are described in more depth on page 87.) A critical element in fostering the involvement of all parents has been the development of an African American parent group separate from the Vaughn Center's predominantly Latino governance commission. African Americans make up a minority of the population in the mostly Latino area surrounding Vaughn. During their time apart, the African American parent group developed an agenda for their school advocacy efforts, which included: 1) fostering bilingualism for all children, 2) developing a curriculum that embraces the cultural richness of the African American community, and 3) ensuring that all children graduate as competent readers. When African American and Latino parents met corporately, the agenda developed by the African American parents allowed parents from both ethnic groups to see where common ground already existed. The Vaughn experience shows how a group's "being apart" can establish the foundation for greater overall unity.

Spending time among members of one's own ethnic group is an important developmental experience.

Recognizing
commonalities is
what helps bind
people together,
builds a greater
sense of commu-
nity, and reduces
stereotypes.

2. Creating Opportunities To Operate In Diverse Settings

To develop understanding among different groups, it is crucial to create programs purposely designed to bring together people of diverse backgrounds to identify and discuss common issues. Consider the approach described by one principal of a Family Resource School in Denver:

> "My sense is some parents were seeing family resource schools as something for other people but not for them... Because we have a wide variety of programs, we have been able to create something for everybody. For example, last year, we had a program called 'Choices,' designed to create time for mothers and daughters to share what it means to grow up, what it means to be an adolescent. The program involved mothers and daughters from very economically impoverished back- grounds to a mother who was an attorney and another parent who had a Ph.D. all working together. It brought them together to see they all had things in common when you are an adolescent. We conscientiously designed program- ming that we thought would be good for both ends of the spectrum."

Embedded in this anecdote is the awareness that recognizing commonalities is what helps bind people together, builds a greater sense of community, and reduces stereotypes. A program such as "Choices" can help affluent parents to see that their counterparts in poorer communities share similar concerns about bringing up children. These types of conversa- tions can also demolish stereotypes, for instance, by demonstrating that wealth does not eradicate problems. Regardless of socioeconomics, the hardships and the joys of mother- daughter relationships during the trials and tribulations of adolescence remain the same.

Conversely, the wealthier mothers could have been alerted to differences, such as the barriers poor parents face in raising children: lack of recreational opportunities in poor neighborhoods; rising concerns over safety in walking to and from school; or the absence of jobs that pay well enough to allow families to support themselves. These insights could be instrumental in helping wealthier parents to understand the importance of supporting programs designed to provide less affluent parents with resources.

Moreover, dialogues between communities about the challenges they face are fruitful ground for identifying problems that require a unified effort and voice to resolve. Commu- nity assessments, as discussed in Chapter 2, provide one strategy for helping diverse constituencies to recognize common interests. But programming allows the development of mechanisms for maintaining a continuous, vibrant dialogue.

At many service sites that California Tomorrow visited, particularly those operating in a school-linked context, one of the most common issues that bound diverse parents together were concerns about improving academic opportunities for their children. Patsy Roybal, the family resource coordinator at Cheltenham Elementary School, says:

> "We believe that we all have to go forward in the same direction. We cannot do that unless you bring the Anglos, the Spanish-speaking Mexican people, and the English-speaking Hispanics together to understand our differences and...to respect that diversity. And not to expect any one of us to give it up but to join in and all focus...toward the betterment of our students."

Other Considerations

In the discussion about fostering group consciousness, as well as communication among diverse groups, a question arises: How should programs create opportunities for participants to have separate as well as integrated experiences? Should such opportunities occur sequentially or simultaneously?

The answers probably lie with the community being served. In some communities, a separate dialogue should come first to give people the clarity and strength needed to participate in an integrated dialogue. (See Building Strength Through Afrocentrism below)

Some communities, however, may have already had opportunities for such dialogue to occur and as a result have people who are well-prepared to enter into discussions with other groups. It is important to recognize, however, that people often feel differing levels of comfort in assuming various roles. Meeting in separate groups still may be helpful even if people are comfortable in an integrated setting. Given the diversity within ethnic groups, it may always be necessary to give separate groups time to clarify common assumptions, beliefs and concerns.

One final thought: while we have described the importance of fostering a sense of identity primarily in terms of ethnic groups, this approach has broader applications. Depending upon the community and the experiences of individuals participating in an initiative, it may be important to allow various types of groups to evolve along lines such as gender, age, or class. Having people participate in multiple groups helps them to see beyond their stereotypes and develop a richer, less categorical understanding of the world.

INTERVIEW

Building Strength Through Afrocentrism

 Located in a predominantly African-American neighborhood in St. Louis, Missouri, the Caring Communities Programs aim to restore a sense of hope and pride in the children and families served and to establish strong neighborhood and family support systems. The integrated services reform effort is a demonstration site of a statewide initiative sponsored by four Missouri state agencies and the Danforth Foundation.

Khatib Waheed, a long-time community resident and director of the Caring Communities Programs since their inception in 1989, was interviewed by California Tomorrow's Hedy Chang, co-author of this report. Waheed talked about the challenges facing African Americans as they attempt to shed the damaging effects of racism and redefine themselves as a strong, support-ive community. Only then, Waheed says, can they tackle the tough but important task of building connections to other groups.

HC: How have you seen issues around race, language, culture and class arise in your work with Caring Communities?

KW: We have to look in a very sensitive way at how both our staff and our customers have been directly and/or indirectly affected by racism; how we have as a people, a staff, and a community, internalized the whole notion of inferiority and powerlessness. We have to redirect, redefine and rethink how we perceive ourselves and what we see ourselves as being able to realistically accomplish...and have the courage, skills and know-

Continued on page 42

how to make those changes. That is a difficult process. On one hand, we have to raise the issue of how racism is practiced, supported and internalized. At the same time, we have to do it in a way that doesn't contribute to a kind of reverse-hatred mentality. We have to look at it in a healthy way.

This is not easy. As a nation, we don't talk about racism well. Too many of us personalize this experience and its definition. Groups often are precluded from getting to the real core of the issue. The core is so shrouded with the emotions, the psychological issues and the scars of racism. It's a constant struggle to get people to understand that we can determine our own destiny; that we should define ourselves as opposed to allowing the media or some other philosophically driven notion to define us. We have to re-establish support systems in our community which are sensitive to our particular needs, origins, experiences and history.

HC: When you say 'we,' to whom are you referring?

KW: I'm talking about African Americans. I don't separate myself from that group. I'm saying 'we' — as staff, as advisory board, as customers, as recipients of those services, as partners in that process of service delivery — need to learn how to redefine ourselves, to determine our own destiny in ways that include other groups and recognize the roles and contributions of other groups, and not to develop a separatist kind of mentality.

HC: Are you trying to create a dialogue within your own community, or is that also a dialogue between African Americans and other groups?

KW: It's not so much a dialogue between African Americans and other groups. I'll tell you why: At this point, it's a strategic or tactical issue. Quite often, given the limitations of time and space, we spend so much time in discussions with other groups around this issue that we never deal with the internal therapy which needs to happen amongst African Americans. We must first learn how to deal with how we — African Americans, their families, and so forth — have internalized racism. Then at some point, we can engage in some healthy dialogue

with other groups. No one is going to do it for us but us. We want a foundation, with our families and within our communities, so that everyone is comfortable once the discourse begins between groups or among groups. The comfort level needs to be high enough so that the result isn't our turning back with our tails tucked between our legs, never wanting to continue the discourse.

HC: How do you go about creating that dialogue?

KW: Right now, we are introducing concepts — introducing the whole notion of Afrocentricity, and helping folks to understand how it is applied practically. One of the mistaken assumptions that is often made about African Americans is that we are a monolithic people — that we all kind of think the same way and dress the same way; all of us 'got rhythm.' It's not true. Some of us are very conservative and could easily become Republicans; some of us are Republicans. Some of us are Democratic in our views. Some of us are very spiritual; some of us are not. Some of us are family-oriented; some are not. Some support notions of separatism; many of us do not. All of us don't relate to Minister Farrakhan or Al Sharpton or Jesse Jackson; some of us don't relate to any national leaders. Some of us are not even movement-oriented. There's a tremendous amount of diversity among us, so the struggle right now is for us to find a common perspective.

HC: What does that mean for your own practice?

KW: We use the seven principles or pillars called *"Nguzo Saba"* in Swahili. They are seven specific concepts that speak to unity, self-determination, and collective work and responsibility, cooperative economics, purpose and creativity, faith. What we're doing is establishing a common acceptance of those values. Consider, for example, a community which, by and large, has accepted *umoja* and *kujichagulia*, the concepts of unity and self-determination. If a person decides to sell dope to the community, then it is on the basis of acceptance of those principles that we can begin to debate whether or not drug trafficking is in the best interests of our community. Instead of limiting the discourse to discussions around what is legal and what is not, we can debate it on a higher plane in terms of what is right, what is just. That's a never-ending, constantly unwinding process.

Another part is to develop specific programming that makes it possible for the free-flowing discussion of those concepts, as well as practical ways of implementing them. So, for example, on the third Friday of every month, we attempt to bring together all of the families who are receiving clinical services to begin to build a family/community support system. We acquaint them in more detail with that (Afrocentric) value system and then begin to use those principles as a focal point to discuss specific issues, such as violence and drug trafficking.

We might say to the parents, 'There's a need for us to find alternative methods to resolving conflicts, other than the use of violence.' One of the practical approaches is to train folks on how to use a more peaceful conflict resolution process, and then link families together who are attempting to follow that process. For example, suppose there are three families on a particular city block receiving services from Caring Communities and have all bought into this notion of peaceful conflict resolution. Then, we begin to encourage those three families to interact more regularly: to allow their children to play amongst themselves; to work together on car pooling to the laundromat, the grocery store; whatever meets their needs. We would facilitate that process of interaction. In doing so, we begin to establish an alternative to the violence. Then we also attempt to engage other families from that block. But if for a long time period, there are no other families on that block who are willing to participate, we would unite those three families with families on other blocks. In other words, it's a matter of starting where you are, but constantly using *Nguzo Saba* as a referent to describe, define and discuss whatever the issues may be.

Our approach is based in those values, which have a specific meaning to African Americans, because the terms are in Swahili. We also talk about Swahili as a language — why it evolved, the parts of the continent where it is used — and begin to talk about the history and cultures of those particular people. At some point, we also have to talk about why it's necessary for us to

couch these terms in our language. So we have to gently talk about the issue of racism; we have to talk about what that has done to us and how we have internalized the self-hatred. Right now, what's most important for the family is, how do they get their kid to go to school? How do you get some clothes on their back? How do you get the mother to stop abusing drugs and abusing the children? You have to inject these discussions when it is appropriate.

HC: What is the connection between this approach to building community and efforts to integrate and reform services?

KW: Cultural diversity is integrated into the process, just as an integrated service delivery process is integrated.

HC: Why do you think it is important to begin engaging other groups in a dialogue about diversity?

KW: First of all, to lower barriers. It's not just about getting African Americans to feel good about being African American. It's more importantly about moving beyond that, understanding that there are more people in the world other than just African Americans. And we have to learn how to appreciate other cultures just as we're struggling to appreciate our own and struggling to get others to appreciate ours. We have to find ways in which we can all live and work interdependently on this planet. Essentially, that's the purpose — so that we can live in peace.

New Strategies for Working with Diverse Children and Families

CHAPTER 4

Equipping Agency Staff to Work with Diverse Populations

New approaches to working with diverse families, as described in the previous chapter, cannot be implemented unless service providers have adequate skills and knowledge. This chapter discusses how agencies can ensure that staff is equipped through staff development and hiring practices to provide culturally and linguistically appropriate services to children and families. It also describes the new forms of leadership and management required.

A. Recognize the Limitations of Diversity Training

Many staff people working on initiatives mentioned that they had participated in some type of staff development workshop or training session aimed at addressing diversity. Sometimes the training was part of a program designed specifically to prepare the line staff who would be involved in piloting new forms of service delivery. Some staff participated in training sessions involving all workers at their home agency.

The popularity of cultural diversity training seems to reflect a growing understanding that service providers need to have specific information and strategies about how to work with diverse ethnic populations. Sometimes, providers can glean information from the families themselves, but it is often extremely helpful to have a general understanding of a group's cultural habits beforehand.

Understanding the wide range of individual differences within a group is also crucial to avoid over-generalizing or stereotyping clients from a particular racial background. Every racial term — white, Latino, Asian, Native American or African American — encompasses many nationalities, each with its own cultural characteristics. Cultures can also evolve over time. Consider the situation of African Americans. While many aspects of African American culture can be traced back to various African tribal traditions, it has also been heavily influenced by the experiences of African Americans in the United States, including slavery, racism, and the civil rights movement. Furthermore, these experiences have varied throughout the United States, so African American culture can exhibit significant regional differences.

Differences can also be generational. One cannot assume for example, that many older African Americans are familiar with the community-oriented principles of *Nguzo Saba* described in the interview with Khatib Waheed of the Caring Communities Programs in St. Louis. (See page 41) These principles are part of a more recent movement to reclaim the African American culture.

If stereotypes are not dismantled, service providers are likely to offer inappropriate care, such as assuming incorrectly that a child or family requires assistance, or conversely, failing to identify when someone is in need of help. They also risk misidentifying the source of a

Service providers need to have specific information and strategies about how to work with diverse ethnic populations.

client's difficulties. Troubled by the Asian model minority myth, Khoa Nguyen, formerly a social worker with the Denver Public Schools and presently a member of the Educational Service Team, observes:

"The myth is that all Asian students and families are all doing well and everyone is a student. But that was the generation that was here two years ago. The current group is different. Many have never been to school and have experienced a lot of trauma....The number of kids joining gangs is growing — not because kids want to be in gangs, but because they have few job opportunities, support is limited and they experience racisim. Often, they are isolated within the school and from their community, which often doesn't respect a person unless they are highly educated."

It is not clear that diversity training, as it is currently provided, is adequate to equip staff, who had wide-ranging reactions to such experiences. Many felt the training was extremely helpful, particularly when it gave them specific knowledge about how to work with a particular ethnic group. On the other hand, dissatisfaction with currently available diversity training was quite prevalent. Sometimes, staff felt the training itself stereotyped groups in an attempt to offer insights about their characteristics. In some cases, staff felt the training increased feelings of ethnic polarization. One person we interviewed shared the following:

It is not clear that diversity training, as it is currently provided, is adequate to equip staff.

"We had a cultural competence training on African Americans, and it made everybody mad on our staff. There's a style of trying to get people to learn about another culture which is not one of healing, but one of attacking. I believe that people need to unlearn their racism, but it should be done in a supportive way — without passing judgment."

Such experiences point out several issues. First, there is significant controversy over the content and approach of current cultural diversity training. Second, the quality of training also varies greatly.

What we heard in the field of human services reflected patterns that emerged in another California Tomorrow endeavor, which involved interviewing 48 projects that focused on intergroup relations among students across lines of culture and race. That project uncovered a wide range of assumptions, visions and strategies among the people engaged in developing these programs. In our effort to make sense of this "field," California Tomorrow identified eight different focus areas among these projects that targeted students: 1) developing personal awareness and communication skills, 2) creating strong, connected communities, 3) resolving conflict, 4) unraveling personal prejudice, 5) recognizing institutional oppression, 6) working to change inequities and harmful practices and policies, 7) gathering strength, support and perspective through others who share common experience, and 8) gaining knowledge about human relations in other times, places, and cultures. While many programs focused on one particular area, some attempted to integrate several.[1]

New Helvetia staff worker and teen

---

[1] See Olsen, Laurie, "Mission Imperative" in *California Perspectives Fall 1992*, Volume 3, p. 62-78.

*In order to have a
long-term impact
on practice,
training must
be on-going.*

Whether a particular program helps a group address a specific issue depends upon the design on the training. For example, a group experiencing tensions because members are misinterpreting each other's cultural styles may find that a session about recognizing institutional oppression will not enhance members' ability to work together. By the same token, an organization having difficulty serving a particular population because the institution engages in some type of discriminatory practice is not likely to be helped by exercises that teach staff how to resolve conflicts between ethnic groups.

Finding the appropriate training requires both understanding the nature of the problem(s) being faced and then identifying which training program(s) are designed to address those particular issues. All too often, however, neither the diversity trainers nor the groups who have hired them have a clear understanding of these dynamics. One consultant we interviewed shared the following:

> "During one seminar held in our county, there was a huge debate among people regarding learning specific kinds of things that are culturally based as opposed to learning a process of relating and learning. I think there are different approaches, and I personally have the latter. I prefer to listen and learn and have a process by which to establish a relationship and make yourself more responsive. But I think for some people who are extremely prejudiced or have severe stereotypes, they probably have to go through a desensitization program — something more deliberate is required. Maybe it depends on different people and what they need."

One important finding of our interviews is that the diversity training sessions described to us during our site visits seemed to focus on unraveling personal prejudice, recognizing institutional oppression and gaining knowledge about people from particular cultural backgrounds. While they dealt with the need to change individual behavior and increase awareness, they did not appear to help participants use that knowledge in an even more strategic fashion: they did not appear to result in an understanding or deeper discussion of the larger implications of diversity for policies, program design, and institutional practices. We believe this situation reflects the fact that much of the diversity training currently being offered tends to be relatively generic. It is intended for a broad range of audiences and frequently not grounded in the specifics of a particular discipline or institution.

Another pitfall: in order to have a long-term impact on practice, training must be ongoing. One of the dangers of "diversity" training sessions is that human service providers will mistakenly believe that participating in a workshop is enough to equip them to work effectively with ethnically and linguistically diverse populations. Given the tremendous variation among individuals in any particular ethnic group and the evolutionary nature of cultures and traditions, a single session will never suffice in teaching someone all there is to know about a particular culture. The best a workshop can do is give an individual some techniques for continually improving his or her ability to work in ethnically diverse environments. Providing individuals with such skills is important. The rapidly changing demographics of many communities means most people will find themselves in situations where they need to have the ability to work with a family who is from a different ethnic background. It is important to remember, however, that information gained from a single workshop does not replace the knowledge gained from life experiences or institutional reinforcements of non-prejudicial behavior.

Embarking on Diversity Training

Diversity training should not be a one-time occurrence, but rather, an on-going process that fits within the staff development plan of any agency or organization. Training must go beyond simply building multicultural understanding and awareness of racist attitudes. Before starting diversity training:

♦ Bring the entire staff together to discuss why diversity training is needed. What issues, concerns or problems do staff members want to address? What does your organization hope to accomplish through diversity training?

♦ Define specifically the issue(s) that the training should address. Is the purpose of training to:

  • develop personal awareness and communication skills?
  • resolve conflict?
  • unravel personal prejudice?
  • recognize institutional oppression?
  • work to change inequities and harmful practices and policies?
  • gather strength, support and perspective through others who share common experience?
  • gain knowledge about other cultures?
  • other issues?

♦ Make sure the entire staff agrees upon the purpose of the training. Often, staff members will have different definitions of what is needed to "address diversity." Taking time to hear various perspectives will result in a better definition of the issues.

♦ Set a realistic schedule for training. Remember: changing the way people think and act takes time. It will probably take more than a single workshop to eradicate personal prejudice and bring about institutional change.

♦ Ask staff members if they know of good trainers. Invite staff to help select trainers.

♦ Make sure trainers have experience addressing the particular issues your organization has identified.

♦ Get references on trainers. This is a crucial step since quality varies greatly.

♦ Work with the trainers to ensure that they understand the issues facing your organization.

♦ Engage all staff who participated in the training when evaluating its effectiveness.

B. Understand the Importance of Reflective Staffing

Hiring staff who reflect the racial and ethnic background of the communities being served offers a number of irreplaceable benefits. First, these staff people often possess knowledge about the culture, traditions, and behavior patterns of their own ethnic group because they were raised in a manner similar to other group members. When working with families, this type of expertise (understanding the roles of various family members, cultural taboos, the connotations of particular body language) is invaluable to establishing trust, drawing upon family strengths and identifying what service might be most helpful. For example, Cher Vang, a community liaison who works with the Yuba County Coordinated Services Project in California, offers the following insight about how he, a younger man, establishes rapport with Hmong parents:

> "It's a cultural thing. In the Hmong culture, younger kids don't talk to older people. I don't expect to speak over their heads. Most of the time I will talk myself down. And most of the parents will call me 'Son' anyway. That's why I can calm the parents down. I don't yell at them the way the [white] Americans do."

By speaking in a respectful manner, Cher Vang avoids offending the older Hmong and opens the door for a productive discussion of the issues affecting their children.

Second, sharing a particular racial or ethnic background helps staff to be more sensitive to particular issues because there is a high likelihood that they have faced similar situations. Such staff may identify issues earlier than staff who have not had similar experiences. For example, one Asian social worker we interviewed voiced his concern that the teachers in a school — none of whom are Asian — rarely referred Asian students to the school-linked services program until just before they were about to graduate to the next grade level. At that late stage, the teachers had suddenly noticed that the Asian students were falling far behind grade level in their reading. In such a situation, a staff worker who shares the ethnic background of the students can be an invaluable resource. By not accepting the "model student" myth, s/he can better spot early warning signs and identify family members who may be able to support the students.

Santa Ana School District administrator Lucinda Hundley was involved in the efforts of one school-linked services initiative to hire staff who reflected the cultures and languages of the families served, in this case, Latinos, African Americans and Asians in Santa Ana. She says:

> "We were deliberate in wanting to hire staff that were of the culture and language of the dominant [Latino] community. Three of our five social workers are of the dominant [Latino] culture and of the dominant language [Spanish] of our parent population. If we could have had an Asian staff member, we would. Our coordinator is African American. She brings the sensitivity based on her own experiences as a minority, and has almost an intuitive sense of how to address issues of diversity."

This reference to the sensitivity of the African American coordinator also demonstrates that sharing similar experiences — such as racial discrimination — can increase a person's awareness of the challenges facing other minority groups.

Third, appearance matters. When people see a staff person from their ethnic background, it is often taken as a favorable indicator of how well a program responds to their concerns. In fact, some administrators told California Tomorrow that hiring an African

American was *critical* to assuring African Americans in their communities that the programs would be responsive to their needs. Jacob Moody, director of the Balboa High School Teen Health Clinic in San Francisco, said,

> "We couldn't deliver services without a multiethnic staff. The kids need to see someone with whom they can identify, someone who pulls them in."

Conversely, the absence of staff from a particular ethnic group, despite its large representation in a community, can create suspicions of discrimination by the employer. Staff who reflect the ethnicity of the community also serve as important role models for children and youth — living proof that success is possible.

In several sites we visited, concerns over staff ethnicity became most intense during the process of selecting a director. To some extent, these concerns mirror the ones raised above. But in the case of choosing a director, fundamental issues of power arise. Hiring a white director to run a program that serves mainly ethnic minorities can be interpreted as simple replication of larger societal patterns of inequitably distributed power and resources. The situation is exacerbated if those who make the hiring decision also fail to reflect the ethnicity of the community being served.

On the other hand, it is important to recognize that appearances can be deceiving. Sometimes people fail to make crucial distinctions between ethnic groups perceived by the larger society to fall under the same broad racial category. For example, at one site we visited, we heard about how the police department hired a Mien police officer in recognition of the need to reach out to a burgeoning Southeast Asian community. But most of the families in the area are Hmong, who had a history of conflict with the Mien while both groups were in Asia. The Hmong would have an extremely difficult time trusting a Mien officer.

Similarly, service providers often do not realize that Latinos and African Americans also represent a wide range of ethnicities. Thus, those working with new or unfamiliar ethnic groups must ask questions and seek advice rather than make assumptions. In the case of the Hmong, some preliminary inquiries to a Hmong community leader or a community-based organization that serves them may have resulted in a more appropriate choice of officers.

Finally, hiring and retaining staff who reflect the racial and ethnic background of the client community can improve families' abilities to access and use services, therefore contributing to better outcomes. Staffing is not the only factor in improving outcomes for families, but it is an extremely important one.

Hiring ethnically and linguistically reflective staff was a major concern of all seven collaborative program sites that California Tomorrow visited. We also surveyed 98 collaborative efforts in the state. We used survey information to assess how frequently these programs, in general, were hiring people who reflected the racial and linguistic backgrounds of the children and families served. If a collaborative indicated that it served a particular racial group, we assessed whether or not it employed at least one staff person from that same racial background.

Our results showed that the large majority of collaborative programs serving whites or Latinos had at least one staff person of the same racial background. However, the match was less successful for other racial/ethnic groups. While 67% of the programs served African Americans, only 33% had at least one African American staff person. Asian/Pacific Islanders were served by 53% of the programs, but only 26% had at least one Asian/Pacific Islander staff person. Native American staff were virtually non-existent. (See Figure 1)

Hiring staff who reflect the racial background of the community can improve families' abilities to access and use services, therefore contributing to better outcomes.

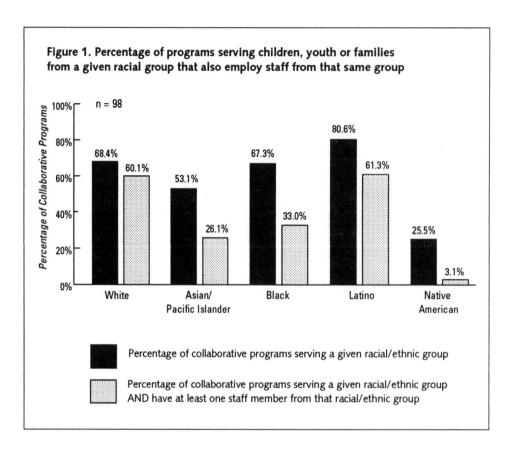

Figure 1. Percentage of programs serving children, youth or families from a given racial group that also employ staff from that same group

n = 98

Percentage of collaborative programs serving a given racial/ethnic group

Percentage of collaborative programs serving a given racial/ethnic group AND have at least one staff member from that racial/ethnic group

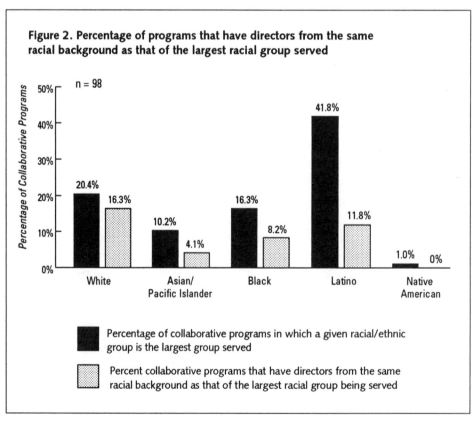

Figure 2. Percentage of programs that have directors from the same racial background as that of the largest racial group served

n = 98

Percentage of collaborative programs in which a given racial/ethnic group is the largest group served

Percent collaborative programs that have directors from the same racial background as that of the largest racial group being served

We also investigated whether collaboratives tended to hire directors from the same racial background as that of the largest racial group being served. Again, the results varied by group. (See Figure 2) Of the 20 collaboratives in which whites made up the largest racial group, 16 of the directors were white. Of the 16 programs in which African Americans predominated, 8 employed directors who were African American. Of the 10 collaboratives serving mostly Asians, only 4 had Asian directors. The greatest discrepancy occurred for Latinos. Of 41 collaboratives that named Latinos as the largest ethnic group served, only 12 had Latino directors.

Note: The authors would like to acknowledge the limitations of the terms "race" and "racial" and the controversy over precisely which ones are appropriate (e.g. Hispanic vs. Latino, or white vs. Anglo). Use of the term "race" is often criticized because it implies a clear-cut biological basis for making a distinction that science has failed to prove. The term also fails to acknowledge the growing number of biracial or multiracial people in American society. These terms do, however, reflect the way our society currently tends to categorize people. In our original survey, we asked collaborative Programs for the specific ethnicity as well as general racial background of children/families and staff. But many respondents were unable to indicate specific ethnic backgrounds. Consequently, when we conducted our analysis, we have found it necessary to rely upon the broad, socially constructed racial categories originally used by the census: white, Latino, Asian Pacific Islander, African American and Native American. While we recognize that race is not the same as ethnicity, this report does assume that race serves as a general indicator of a person's ethnic and cultural background.

C. Look Beyond Race and Ethnicity

Hiring staff who reflect the community remains critical. But it is also important to keep in mind that race and ethnicity are only part of the equation. The fact that a staff person originates from the same ethnic background as a particular group offers no guarantee that he or she knows how to work with such clients. Culture is not just a function of race and ethnicity, but is influenced by many factors, including level of acculturation to mainstream society and socioeconomic status. One Latina administrator we interviewed shared the following story:

> "I know of a program which was founded and administered by a young, attractive American-born woman who looks Mexican but is not fluent in Spanish. Real gaps exist between her and the immigrant moms with whom she works. These women, who are mostly Spanish speakers and housewives, have had very different life experiences. Although this woman has contributed a lot in terms of resources, she just does not fit in. As the founder and chief fundraiser of the organization, she expects to be treated as a leader and be praised for her efforts. However, the other mothers think she is very "aggressive;" they are threatened by her looks and manner. Rather than opening their arms to her, the mothers have bonded together and closed her out."

Likewise, several people we interviewed said that they have seen some of the most alienating, condescending behavior towards minorities exhibited by those of the same ethnic background, but of higher class or professional status. One white administrator with a strong community organizing background asserted:

> "Culture and language is not just a matter of ethnic background; it is also a matter of your profession or system. Let me see if I can say this without being offensive: Is a professional black mental health worker more culturally competent with a black, southeast San Diego drug dealer than I am? Part of me says no — that a black or Hispanic middle-class person with a professional degree has their own cultural disconnects — particularly if they have never lived in a barrio or a very low-income area. We have yet to learn to talk about differences among economic culture, family culture, ethnic culture, or the culture of a particular country or how all of them intermingle."

When a staff person comes from a different racial background than a client, establishing trust often requires compassion and perseverance.

Instead of race or ethnicity, a better sign of common cultural heritage is whether a staff person grew up in the same geographic community under similar economic conditions as the children and families served. During our site visits, we found that individuals who fit this description were tremendous assets. An excellent example is Glen Harris, Yuba County probation officer and staff coordinator of the Yuba County Coordinated Service Council, an initiative that primarily targets poor white children. Like the youngsters, Harris is also white, but the reason he has good rapport with them stems more from his socioeconomic background and local ties. Honest and hardworking, Harris is the product of a poor, white working-class family that, like many others in the community, originally migrated to California from the Oklahoma dustbowl. He has dwelled in Yuba County all his life. Having lived in poverty and worked in the fields, Harris is intimately aware of the challenges facing many of the children in his program. Rather than condemning them for coming to school dirty or smelly, Harris points out that many live in homes without running water or washing machines. He worries that teachers who do not understand students' home conditions sometimes say things that degrade the children in front of their peers. At the same time, Harris' intimate knowledge of the community allows him to tap into his informal network of friends and resources for help.

On the other hand, while shared cultural heritage or similar socioeconomic/geographical backgrounds can be very important, absence of these factors does not indicate that a person will be unable to develop a healthy helping relationship with a child or family. Rachel Lodge, director of the California Healthy Start Field Office, says:

> "Obviously if I share a family's cultural background, I will have a much better appreciation for what they're about. If I don't, then I need to learn a lot more. Depending on how close their experience is to my own, it's going to take a shorter or longer amount of time to understand their issues. From the family's perspective, it is easier if I am familiar to them. But I guess I'd like to think that, regardless of whether one is from the group, it's possible to work together effectively."

When a staff person comes from a different racial background than a client, establishing trust often requires compassion and perseverance. One Latina project director told us:

> "Though we say that we can work with everyone, the reality is that people have those with whom they feel more comfortable. I have had to work hard to prove myself to the four African American parents who are working here because they were checking me out all the time. I went into a period of being tested — whether I was about what I was saying I was about."

Another consultant we interviewed, Katherine Armstrong, has had similar experiences. When she began helping one predominantly minority community to develop a plan for reforming services to children and families, she claims she immediately felt a great deal of distrust from them. Reflecting back to the situation she said, "I looked like a stereotypical white person. I felt that people were questioning my right to be in the room." Nonetheless, Armstrong felt that over time, she was able to build trust by being honest about the situation and not taking offense, an approach she felt was crucial:

> "I was comfortable acknowledging my status. I would ask, 'Would the community be comfortable having a white person do this?' Second, I was persistent; I just didn't go away. So often, the community has seen people come to their community to get something from them and then disappear. Third, I tried to listen and only give information that was pertinent or relevant. I tried not to give unsolicited advice. And then I did a lot of work on their behalf. I wrote proposals; I made connections with other programs; I followed through on assignments — I tried to provide a lot of support."

All individuals who work with families need to establish bonds of trust across gaps of culture and race.

In many ways, all individuals who work with families need to be prepared to establish bonds of trust across gaps of culture and race. Even when an organization has diverse staff, it may not always be possible or desirable to match staff and families by ethnicity.

Sometimes, a family may prefer to work with a staff member from a different ethnic background. For example, a child or teen might like to talk to an adult about an extremely sensitive issue, such as drug abuse or an unwanted pregnancy. The young person might believe that confidentiality can be better safeguarded if he or she works with someone from a different background. Perhaps a youth or a family might simply be more comfortable with a staff member of a different background because of personal characteristics, such as style of interaction or particular expertise. Whether a client prefers being assigned to a service provider of the same ethnic heritage depends on a wide range of factors, including how comfortable the client feels about operating in a cross-cultural context.

Two sites we visited allowed clients to indicate whether they preferred to work with a staff person of the same ethnic background — a choice that makes services more consumer-driven. (See Sacramento profile on page 65)

One issue worth further exploration is how much the nature of the service should influence matching of ethnicity or cultural awareness between a worker and a family. For example, employing a worker steeped in the cultural and linguistic nuances of a particular ethnic group may be crucial if the job entails home visits. But in other situations, it may be more important to find a person with a certain set of technical skills (e.g. knowledge of medical procedures) than to find someone who shares the family's cultural background.

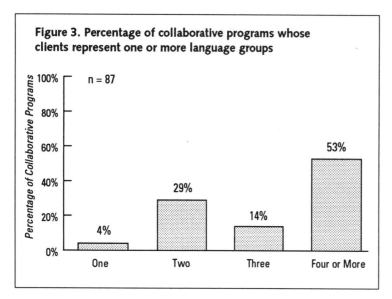

Figure 3. Percentage of collaborative programs whose clients represent one or more language groups

n = 87

- One: 4%
- Two: 29%
- Three: 14%
- Four or More: 53%

Percentage of Collaborative Programs

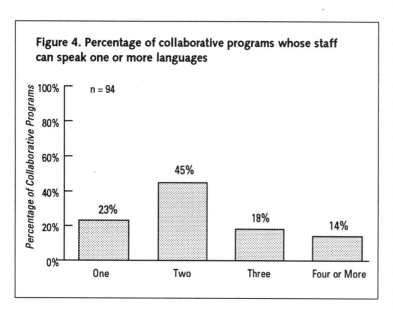

Figure 4. Percentage of collaborative programs whose staff can speak one or more languages

n = 94

- One: 23%
- Two: 45%
- Three: 18%
- Four or More: 14%

Percentage of Collaborative Programs

D. Don't Underestimate the Critical Importance of Language

The ability of staff to communicate directly with children, youth and families is crucial. Without a common language, families cannot ask questions or raise concerns. Nor can staff easily assess client needs and resources or provide advice. Therefore, employers who hire staff who reflect the clients' ethnicities must also make a conscientious effort to find workers who speak the clients' languages as well. Ethnicity, culture, and language are integrally connected, but they are not interchangeable.

According to our survey of collaborative programs, only 4% serve clients who speak English only. The other 96% serve clients who speak languages other than English. Of these programs, some had two to three languages represented among their clientele. But significantly, a majority of programs serve four or more language groups. (See Figure 3) For almost all collaboratives, commitment to providing clients with access to services requires that staff members be able to work in multilingual settings.

But clearly, more strides need to be made in hiring bilingual staff. Only 14% of the collaboratives surveyed had staff who collectively spoke four or more languages; 18% had staff who spoke three or more languages; 45% had staff who spoke two or more languages, and among 23% only one language was spoken by staff. (See Figure 4)

Given this shortage of bilingual staff, it is hardly surprising that many collaboratives reported language barriers as a significant communication problem. Of the 88 programs that responded to the survey question about language obstacles, a vast majority, 91%, indicated some difficulty in communicating with youth because these clients spoke a language other than English. Almost one out of five programs said they had trouble communicating with half or more of the children they serve. (See Figure 5)

Language barriers are even more serious for parents. When the survey asked collaboratives if they ever had difficulty communicating with parents because these clients spoke a language other than English, 95% of responding programs said yes. (See Figure 6) Furthermore, 40% of programs estimated that language barriers existed with one-quarter to one-half of parents; 29% of programs reported difficulty in communicating with half or more of the parents served.

Other than English, the languages most commonly spoken by children and families were Spanish, Vietnamese, Cambodian, Chinese, Tagalog, Hmong and Korean. Ability to work

Drawing Strength from Diversity

with families in their home language varied according to linguistic group. Faring best were collaboratives that served Spanish speakers: 69% percent of these programs employed at least one Spanish-speaking staff person. In contrast, fewer than 15% of the collaboratives that served other minority language groups had any staff who could speak that same tongue. (See Figure 7 on page 56)

Too many agencies underestimate the importance of employing or training professionals who can communicate directly with families in their native tongues. Instead, agencies often rely on translators. But in many cases, translation may not be enough to assist a non-English speaking family to the fullest. Conversations may involve specialized terms unfamiliar to the translator. The presence of a third party can impede a professional's ability to put a family at ease, particularly if confidential information is being sought. As described in the profile of San Diego New Beginnings on page 91, hiring culturally appropriate staff who speak clients' home languages is critical to effective outreach and service delivery.

Sometimes staff members try to overcome a language barrier by asking a youngster to translate for his or her parents. But this tactic can involve the child in what should be strictly an adult discussion and thereby exacerbate an already stressful power imbalance within the family. Many immigrant parents find themselves losing their authority once they arrive in the U.S. because they are forced to rely upon their children, who have adapted much more quickly to the language and culture. Furthermore, as illustrated by one of the scenarios that open this report, youngsters may not always be reliable translators.

While the ideal is to employ a professional who speaks the home language of the family, this may not always be possible, given the diversity of languages spoken. Inevitably, many human service organizations will need to continue relying upon translators. Those who do so, however, should heed the importance of finding qualified translators because good translation is an acquired skill that transcends fluency in two languages. Lucy Trujillo, Project Coordinator of the Denver Family Resource Schools, explains:

> "An effective translator becomes a partner with the families for whom she translates....If she comes across as too professional and alienates the family, there is no trust or bonding and there is still a gap between systems and the family."

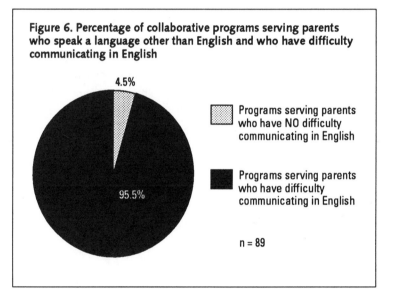

Figure 5. Percentage of collaborative programs serving children and youth who speak a language other than English and who have difficulty communicating in English

9.1%

90.9%

Programs serving children and youth with NO difficulty communicating in English

Programs serving children and youth who have difficulty communicating in English

n = 88

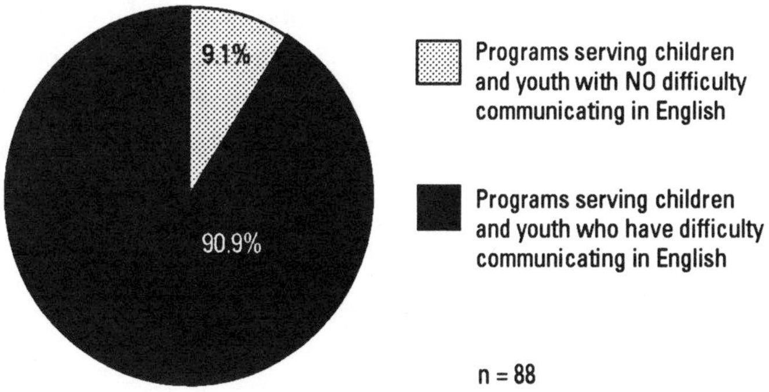

Figure 6. Percentage of collaborative programs serving parents who speak a language other than English and who have difficulty communicating in English

4.5%

95.5%

Programs serving parents who have NO difficulty communicating in English

Programs serving parents who have difficulty communicating in English

n = 89

While it is often appropriate for translators to restate the provider's question in a more sensitive manner, they must take great care to translate the family's response accurately. Translators must not impede the professionals' work by failing to pass critical information along to the family or by giving professionals their interpretation of a situation rather than an exact translation of what a family has said. The accompanying list on page 58 offers tips on how agencies can use translators effectively.

In addition, an agency's translated written materials should be age- and reading-level appropriate, as well as culturally appropriate. One way to ensure that translations are idiomatic and accurate is to have one person translate the materials from English to the other language, then have a second person translate back into English.

E. Provide Leadership to Address Diversity

As the preceding sections demonstrate, making changes at the line staff level is critical to ensuring that services are appropriate for diverse populations. However, it is important to move beyond line staff to the heads of agencies, who play crucial leadership roles. Because top administrators set the vision and atmosphere for their departments, they can give a clear signal that diversity is important through their words and actions. Without their leadership, innovative efforts to provide culturally and linguistically appropriate services may not succeed due to opposition from mid-managers or line staff. For example, Penelope Clarke, Sacramento County Director of Human Assistance, played a critical leadership role in ensuring that all managers and line staff went along with new and highly controversial special skills job classifications for language and culture. (See Sacramento County profile on page 65) Along with leadership skills, administrators must also have the management skills to work with a diverse staff.

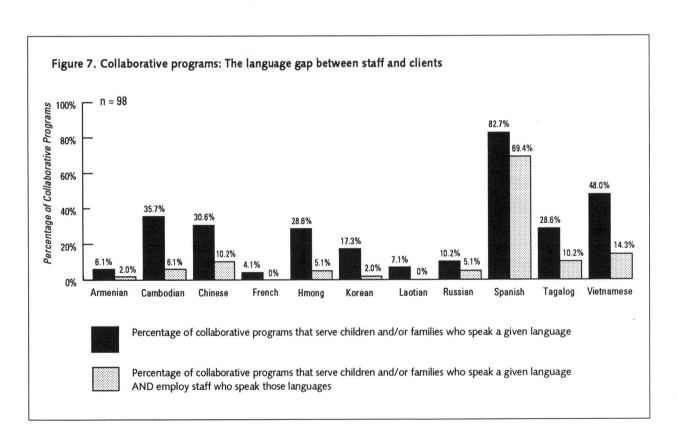

Figure 7. Collaborative programs: The language gap between staff and clients

Percentage of Collaborative Programs

n = 98

■ Percentage of collaborative programs that serve children and/or families who speak a given language

▒ Percentage of collaborative programs that serve children and/or families who speak a given language AND employ staff who speak those languages

F. Equip Administrators to Promote Diversity

Equipping administrators with the skills to manage a diverse staff is a pressing issue. Although staffing in collaborative programs is not yet fully reflective of the communities served, it has already become relatively diverse. Eighty-five percent of the collaborative programs surveyed employ staff from two or more ethnic groups. (See Figure 8)

This staff diversity has significant implications for how an organization is administered and managed. It calls for all administrators — agency heads and mid-level managers — to develop skills to: 1) draw upon the strengths of diverse employees, and 2) promote cross-cultural understanding among staff.

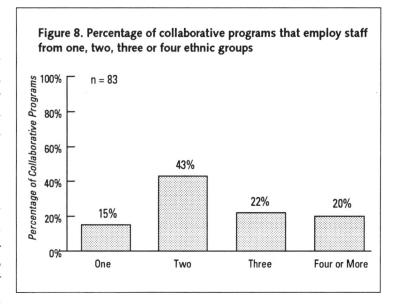

Figure 8. Percentage of collaborative programs that employ staff from one, two, three or four ethnic groups

It is important to emphasize that mid-managers also need to develop these abilities. Mid-managers are often overlooked in discussions to reform systems, even though they are responsible for overseeing line staff, programs and services. Failure to pay attention to the role of mid-managers in creating change can result in their resistance to new approaches taken by line staff. The following section discusses how mid-managers and agency heads can promote diverse strengths and cross-cultural understanding within their departments.

1. Recognize and Draw Upon Diverse Strengths

Administrators who hope to foster culturally appropriate services must promote the sharing of staff members' various knowledge and strengths. But it is not easy to establish an environment in which diverse staff can teach each other how to work effectively with different ethnic populations, as well as alert co-workers to possible cultural taboos. Diversity creates new and different demands on administrators and managers. Without leadership and commitment, staff is left to struggle individually to infuse diversity into the organizational agenda. Such situations can lead to burn-out and resentment on the part of staff who take the initiative to increase the agency's responsiveness.

For managers, a diverse staff often means that a single approach to getting a job done no longer exists. When a Latina pays a home visit to a Latino family, she is likely to ask different questions and attune to different issues than her African American colleague who visits an African American home.

Both workers' effectiveness in establishing rapport is directly related to the fact that they adopt different approaches. When Steve Hamai of the East Bay Asian Youth Center served as the manager of the Real Alternatives Program, a multiethnic collaborative aimed at drug and alcohol prevention, he found that:

> "As a manager, I had to be able to trust that my staff was doing their best. I did not believe I could tell my African American or Latino staff about how to work with families from their communities. For many supervisors, this kind of loose managerial role feels extremely uncomfortable."

When diversity is the norm, managers may not always be able to rely on their personal methods to gauge whether a staff person is relating to clients in an appropriate manner. Instead, managers could develop new systems of assessment in which staff members are evaluated by results, as opposed to whether they adhered to a particular approach. In this case, the outcome should be mutually agreed upon and clearly understood. Such a system can allow staff the flexibility to determine the most appropriate approach. Other strategies include assessing whether clients' access to and utilization of services has increased and regularly asking clients for their evaluations of workers.

2. Promote Cross-Cultural Understanding

Staff members, by virtue of their diversity, often define job responsibilities and appropriate professional behavior in differing ways. Some may think efficiency and speed are essential to any task, while others believe it is more important to focus on the relationship-building

---

Ideas for Working Effectively with Translators

♦ Orient translators to your program's philosophy and purpose.

♦ Let the translator know how your agency wants families to be treated: with respect, without judgment, etc.

♦ Be sure the translator understands the importance of accurately translating information provided by the family, without softening or editing it.

♦ Be aware that a single language (e.g. Chinese) can often encompass several dialects. Make sure the translator is fluent in the specific dialect spoken by the client.

♦ Review any technical terms with the translator to make sure s/he understands and is prepared to translate them.

♦ Inform the translator of the meeting's purpose and of any potentially sensitive topics that may arise.

♦ Ask the translator whether s/he is concerned about the cultural appropriateness of any of the information or questions to be translated, particularly if sensitive topics, such as abuse, severe illness or sexuality will be discussed. Work with the translator to figure out how to best present that information to the family.

♦ Be aware of situations in which information of a sensitive nature would make it inappropriate to use a translator who is a family member, or is of the opposite sex, or a different age. If in doubt, ask the family if they would feel comfortable with a particular person translating.

♦ Allow time for the translator to establish rapport with the family.

♦ Debrief with the translator after speaking with the family.

---

aspects of a particular activity. Or staff may have different ideas about how concerns should be communicated. While some cultures tend to rely upon overt expression of their feelings, others may emphasize more understated approaches. Unchecked, these differences of opinion and misunderstandings can create tension and resentment among staff.

How administrators and managers handle potential misunderstandings has a powerful impact on the overall climate of an office. Consider the experience related to us by one manager:

> "During one staff meeting, the discussion started getting a little heated. One of the African American staff was really pushing for a confrontation. The two Latinos — we were both approaching it from a very different perspective. But, I didn't say, 'Because you're black, this is how you want to approach it.' I said, 'Because we're Latino, it's interesting that it's the two Latinas who are looking for a more diplomatic way to deal with this. It may be that our cultural style is not comfortable with the approach that's being recommended.' But it is hard. I really felt that I was stepping out on a limb, but I felt that I had to make something clear so that people weren't feeling attacked personally. I had to point out that maybe we just had different levels of comfort with different strategies because of our cultures."

Recognizing these issues, Connie Busse, director of the New Beginnings Center at San Diego's Hamilton Elementary School, feels it is her responsibility to foster an atmosphere of respect and acceptance among her multiethnic, multidisciplinary staff. She creates opportunities for staff members to discuss their backgrounds in ways that honors each of their traditions. For example, during staff lunches, she encourages employees to talk about their lives and and how each person's culture and upbringing have shaped them. Such discussions are a non-threatening, enjoyable strategy for giving staff greater insight into why their co-workers hold particular beliefs or act in certain ways.

Despite the most thoughtful leadership, conflict and misunderstandings are still bound to occur within organizations. Therefore, creating forums to help staff better understand one another, as well as developing group norms for promoting constructive discussions, are crucial elements for helping a diverse staff work as a team to serve children, youth and families. (See Guidelines for Managing Conflict in Diverse Organizations on page 60)

The ability to discuss and resolve conflicts is a critical element of effective management in any organization. But it is perhaps even more important when a diverse group is engaged in an effort to reform human services. These reforms dramatically alter how agencies have typically operated. By themselves, such changes can create confusion and ambiguity for staff. Racial, cultural and linguistic diversity, as well as differing professional backgrounds, add another layer of complexity. In this ambiguous atmosphere, managers need to work with staff in discerning whether problems stem from racial or cultural roots, differing professional perspectives, or are related to other types of organizational changes. Sometimes, problems reflect a combination of these factors. Determining the source(s) of a conflict is essential to developing an appropriate solution.

One final consideration remains in equipping agencies to work with multicultural populations: diversifying agency leadership.

Creating forums to help staff better understand one another, as well as developing group norms for promoting constructive discussions, are crucial elements for helping a diverse staff work as a team.

G. Diversify Management

Diverse leadership provides evidence that the organization truly values the contributions of people from all backgrounds at the highest levels of decision-making.

While the bulk of this chapter has discussed diversity among staff who work directly with families, the importance of diversity at all organizational levels should not be underestimated. Ethnic diversity among managers offers a number of benefits.

First, such pluralism can strengthen management by increasing the diversity of management styles. Culture and gender often influence how a person manages an organization (democratic vs. authoritarian; formal vs. informal; emotional vs. stoic.) Some employees respond more positively to one style over another. Some styles are more appropriate in certain situations than others. Having a range of management styles provides the flexibility to handle a wider variety of situations.

Second, ethnic diversity increases the chances that the management team will be able to understand staff issues and concerns. For example, employees who have experienced much racial discrimination are likely to be extremely sensitive to situations in which they believe they are not getting the same treatment as a colleague of a different race, even if the reason behind the differential treatment is absolutely unrelated to race. Managers with similar life experiences can help fellow administrators, who may be less aware, to anticipate and understand these situations.

Third, diverse leadership is an important demonstration of an organization's commitment to diversity. It provides evidence that the organization truly values the contributions of people from all backgrounds, even at the highest levels of decision-making. Moreover, when an effective management team is ethnically diverse, it also models for the staff and the community that power can be shared across racial lines. Ethnically diverse management increases the likelihood that management will have the skills and personal insights to draw upon the strengths of diverse staff and promote cross-cultural understanding.

Guidelines for Managing Confict in Diverse Organizations*

Programs seeking to reform services for children are not alone in attempting to meet the challenges of managing an ethnically diverse staff. Organizations nationwide, from small non-profit agencies to large corporations, are grappling with similar issues.

In the private sector, companies face the challenge of shifting "From Affirmative Action to Affirming Diversity," R. Roosevelt Thomas wrote in the the March/April 1990 issue of the *Harvard Business Review*. To be competitive, he said, companies must move beyond simply hiring a diverse work force to developing managers capable of drawing upon the strengths of those diverse ranks to obtain a better product.

Moreover, when Xerox, one company that Thomas described, began examining how to manage a diverse workforce, a more fundamental problem was discovered: a general lack of skills in managing anyone, much less people who were quite different from oneself.

In the article, "Honoring Diversity: Problems and Possibilities for Staff and Organizations," Marge Carter discussed similar issues in managing child care centers. One approach she suggested for maintaining trust and open lines of communication among diverse staff is to develop a set of agreements on how to handle potential areas of conflict. These agreements can be invaluable in helping staff avoid judgmental, defensive reactions so that criticisms can result in constructive outcomes. Below are the specific points developed by Carter's staff:

Staff Agreements and Approaches to Criticism when Agreements Are Broken

1. We will each have an attitude of flexibility and cooperation in our work here, thinking of the needs of others and the group, along with our own needs.

2. We will each carry a full share of the workload, which includes some extra hours outside our work schedule (e.g. parent conferences, meetings, planning and preparation of activities, recordkeeping, progress reports)

3. We will each communicate directly and honestly with each other. We will be respectful and honorable in our interactions.

4. When problems or difficulties related to our work arise, we will address them rather than ignore or avoid them.

5. We will all be informed of significant problems that affect the program. These will be communicated in person as soon as possible and in writing as necessary.

6. We understand that it is appropriate to seek help from the director on sensitive or difficult issues.

7. When necessary, we will use a criticism/self-criticism decision process to identify attitudes and behaviors that are negatively affecting our agreements.

Criticism/Self-Criticism Process:
To investigate and educate so that we continue to adhere to our agreements.

Questions to ask oneself before giving a criticism:
1. Is my criticism based on investigation or on assumption?
2. What is the most important element of the criticism? Secondary?
3. What is my side of the problem, my responsibility or my contribution to it?
4. What are my disguises that keep me from being criticized?
5. Is my criticism intended to hurt or attack, or is it to educate?
6. How are our agreements hurt or helped by what I am criticizing?
7. How can I play a concrete, positive role in helping the other person change?
8. What changes do I need to make in myself?

Stating a criticism:

When you do...I feel...
It hurts our agreements because...Therefore I want you to...
In the future I will behave differently by...

Investigative discussion of the criticism:

Why do you feel that way? What happened?
What other things were going on? (objective thing happening, feelings)
What is the main thing that needed to happen here?

---

* Reference: Marge Carter, "Honoring Diversity: Problems and Possibilities for Staff and Organizations" in *Alike and Different: Exploring Our Humanity with Young Children.*

CHAPTER 5

The Implications of Diversity for Institutional Change

Often, a charismatic individual uses his or her expertise to improve a program or services. But if such changes are not institutionalized, their impact will be limited, lasting only as long as the charismatic leader's term or confined only to certain activities. In the long run, addressing issues of diversity requires changing institutional policies and practices so that they promote rather than inhibit the development of responsive programs.

Unfortunately, the experiences of many who work with children and families show that new approaches to service delivery, hiring or training often run into barriers imposed by the system. These obstacles range from lack of appropriate pre-service training to limitations created by personnel rules and regulations, to the restrictions of the current fragmented categorical funding streams.

Family Mosaic staff

The current movement to reform systems recognizes the need for institutional change throughout the broad spectrum of agencies that create the current service delivery system. Such agencies range from those that work directly with children and families (e.g. schools, public departments of health, social services or probation) to the institutions that prepare the people employed in those agencies. By arguing that diversity requires re-examination of policies and practices in all sectors, the reform movement offers an opportunity to improve how issues of diversity are addressed.

This chapter examines various types of institutional changes that could promote the provision of culturally and linguistically appropriate services. These include: revamping in-service and pre-service training, re-examining personnel rules and regulations, adopting new strategies for financing services, and fostering continual evaluation of practices through outcomes accountability.

A. Revamp In-Service and Pre-Service Training

Staff development plays an important role in equipping employees to adopt the culturally and linguistically appropriate practices discussed in Chapter 3. Staff development is one of the most frequently used strategies for enhancing skills and expertise.

But the human services field as a whole suffers from the absence of a systematic approach to staff development. Most sites that California Tomorrow visited had specifically designed some form of development for staff members involved in the reform effort. Employees we interviewed generally felt these activities were important in preparing them for their jobs. But it was unclear how these new activities influenced or were coordinated with on-going training within the home agencies of staff reallocated to collaborative efforts. Typically, staff development activities seemed to be created on a site-by-site or ad hoc basis. In order to have a lasting impact, policy-makers and practitioners need to ensure that comprehensive, effective staff development is available to everyone hired to work with children and families.

On-the-job staff development is necessary because workers are not being adequately prepared by the universities and colleges to work in an increasingly multicultural, multi-disciplinary environment. Sid Gardner, director of the Center for Collaboration for Children, reminds us, "The best service integration efforts won't change the system if the universities keep teaching it wrong."

Changing the situation requires going to the root of how all service providers are equipped to do their jobs. Universities and colleges have yet to reform their curricula to ensure that tomorrow's teachers, social workers, nurses, and other service providers have the ability to work with ethnically diverse populations.

In fact, the training that such professionals traditionally have received sometimes increases the likelihood that they will not adopt effective strategies. For example, initiatives experimenting with new forms of service delivery face the common problem of having to help staff overcome the agency and disciplinary biases that lead them to take categorical, rather than holistic, approaches to working with families. Sometimes, these biases also cause staff to discount family members' views, particularly if these clients are from a different cultural background.

Furthermore, interdisciplinary collaboration is widely accepted in theory, but in practice, it requires staff to adopt wholly new ways of making decisions and developing ideas. Sometimes training in a particular discipline makes a staff member feel that s/he alone has the expertise to solve a problem. One should not underestimate the challenge of encouraging professionals to collaborate with others who may have very different ideas about how to best assist families.

Fortunately, growing attention is being paid to pre-service training efforts. Currently, several initiatives housed at various universities, including California State University at Fullerton, the University of Southern California, and the University of Washington, are attempting to transform pre-service preparation for professionals who work with families. These initiatives recognize the importance of preparing professionals to adopt new, cross-disciplinary service strategies. Typical components include: revising the core curriculum, encouraging faculty and students to work together on cross-disciplinary, inter-departmental research projects, and creating student internships at organizations experimenting with new forms of service delivery.

Some of these initiatives also recognize the importance of teaching professionals to work with ethnically diverse populations. Pre-service reform initiatives can promote attention to diversity if they: 1) ensure that the core curriculum teaches students strategies for working in culturally diverse settings, and 2) emphasize recruitment of students from communities that have been traditionally under-represented.

B. Re-Examine the Current System of Personnel Rules, Regulations and Professional Credentials

Staff development and professional preparation are only parts of the equation. Institutions must also re-examine how they make recruitment and hiring decisions. Traditional credentials and hiring requirements can shut out people who may be best suited for a job. Most of the service delivery system is designed to provide supports to low-income and minority communities, but individuals who come from these places often have not had access to the education that would give them the formal qualifications typically required for staff positions.

On one hand, a credential can be an important indicator of whether a person has the skills to do a particular job. For example, most people would agree that it is best to be operated upon by a trained surgeon. On the other hand, sometimes it is debatable whether a credential reflects a person's ability to perform a task. Running an after-school program, listening sympathetically to a young person, or helping a parent identify and gain access to resources are tasks that may be unnecessarily reserved for professionals, such as teachers, psychiatrists or social workers. Uncredentialed people have performed many of these tasks well and sometimes with more sensitivity than their highly credentialed counterparts. At the Vaughn Family Center inside a Los Angeles Unified School District elementary school, parents help other parents to find resources and services. Parents felt it was unnecessary to have a credentialed social worker when they were capable of helping one another.

Clearly, a new balance must be struck between formal credentials and informal qualifications to eliminate barriers against those who can provide linguistically and culturally appropriate care. Reflecting upon her experiences, consultant Katherine Armstrong says:

> "I'm not being naive about how difficult this can be. I know of several situations where community people were hired and they turned out to have drug problems and had to be let go. Sometimes, the community is made up of different factions. This makes it difficult. If you hire from one faction, that person will automatically be dismissed by other groups in the community. But, I do think there always are neutral people. I think there always are competent people. And I think that usually, if you make the right kind of effort, you'll find community leaders to hire. I'm not sure expertise is as important as someone who really understands and is known in the community and is trusted, and can get people to participate."

Changing recruitment and hiring processes is not an easy task. It requires paying close attention to the forces that create the requirements in the first place. Expressing her frustration, one person interviewed said:

> "There are inherent barriers in public service that really affect people's ability to be conscious and responsive to culture and diversity and clients. Those barriers are the rules that are built into the unions' negotiations with the departments, the rules that have to do with civil service. We are recruiting for service integration teams in two communities. For one, I wanted to recruit staff who could represent the new immigrants and the African Americans, and in the other I wanted to draw upon a strong community of Hispanic citizens. But there are all kinds of personnel rules and regulations having to do with qualifications, seniority, limits on the number of people who can be interviewed, that get in the way. With budget constraints, it's really difficult to hire folks from the community."

Reforming the rules that guide how staff are recruited, hired, and rewarded requires dealing with internal personnel regulations as well as union contracts. The experience of Sacramento County demonstrates both the challenges and the benefits of tackling these issues.

"There are inherent barriers in public service that affect people's ability to be conscious and responsive to culture and diversity."

Drawing Strength from Diversity

Sacramento County Language and Culture Job Classifications

Responsiveness to Client Requests

When a client walks into the Sacramento County welfare office, she will be greeted with choices that are unusual in the realm of public agencies. If she speaks a language other than English, she is matched with an eligibility worker or social worker who speaks that same tongue. If she feels more comfortable with someone who understands her cultural background — be it African American, Native American or Mexican — she can request a social worker skilled in working with that specific culture.

This consumer-driven approach of assigning workers based on clients' cultural and linguistic preferences stems from controversial changes to Sacramento employee classifications made nearly two decades ago. These special classifications, which designate social workers capable of working with particular cultural or linguistic groups, have given the welfare department the ability to hire and retain staff capable of serving the county's ethnically diverse population.

The number of job classifications is flexible. New categories are added as the client makeup changes. Currently, the county employs special skills workers to assist clients from the Native American and African American cultures, as well as Chinese, Filipino, Japanese, Mexican/Spanish, Vietnamese, Laotian and Russian languages and cultures. But this form of service was created only after much dissension.

Creation of Language and Culture Job Classifications

The origins of these classifications reach back to the late 1970s. Before the passage of Proposition 13 in 1978, the Sacramento County Welfare Department staffed its operation under the seniority system. In the event of layoffs, those with more years of work

Children and staff at New Helvetia

experience would be retained while those with fewer years would be let go. When Proposition 13 led to budget cuts, the welfare department was forced to lay off workers, beginning with those who had the least seniority. These workers were largely minorities — African American, Latino and Asian.

The impending layoffs split the strong, united union. White workers with greater seniority felt that their years of experience should be recognized and the seniority system maintained. But African American, Latino and Asian workers opposed the seniority system, charging that it would cause a disproportionate number of African Americans and Latinos to be laid off. Chuck Gatten, a former welfare department social worker, recalls those turbulent days with sorrow:

> *"We were a strong union that was broken off in pieces. We were fighting our good brothers and sisters."*

Continued on page 66

The county, on behalf of the minority workers, went to court against the union. The county made two arguments: first, that the union practice of laying off workers solely on the basis of seniority had a disproportionate impact on minority workers who were hired later than white workers; second, that welfare clients had special needs, linguistic and cultural, and deserved to have those needs addressed through appropriate staffing.

The union disagreed bitterly with the county about using culture as the basis for special job classifications. Much of the resistance stemmed from fear; establishing culture as the basis for job categories was, at that point, equivalent to laying off white workers with greater seniority. The union resistance also involved a lot of pride. Many white workers believed that they could work just as effectively as minority workers with clients from different cultures.

Nevertheless, the court ruled in favor of the county. Looking back at that decision, Chuck Gatten believes the court ruled in the best interests of clients:

> "I was initially on the side of the union. But I began questioning when I saw people I respected on the other side. I just came to believe that we were fighting a battle that was artificial. Seniority could not be the sole determinant of meeting client needs. Having the choice is what's important for people. Generally, it makes people comfortable to have someone look like them and it helps them get services."

An important outcome of the lawsuit was development of the job classifications that define skills and abilities for working with particular cultural or linguistic groups. Social workers in these categories must demonstrate their ability to communicate fluently in the required languages. They also must know about the cultural group's family structure, family roles, living environments, and history. The job specifications ask only for the knowledge and skills to work with particular cultures; workers need

not come from the same racial background. Should layoffs arise again, these new job classifications enable the welfare department to retain workers capable of offering culturally and linguistically appropriate services.

Creating the new classifications was only the first step in providing clients with a culturally and linguistically competent staff. The welfare department also had to ensure that qualified workers were actually hired and accepted by other staff.

Today, Penelope Clarke, director of the Department of Human Assistance (the Welfare department's new name), works hard to continue recruiting qualified candidates. Going beyond traditional graduate schools, the department actively recruits in various ethnic communities. Members of internal department caucuses, such as the Latino Caucus, the Asian Caucus, and the Coalition Against Racism (the African American caucus) also help recruit. The department will hire on a provisional basis certain candidates with the potential to perform well, but who have difficulties with the written exam. During this period, the department provides on-the-job training and classes for improving test-taking skills. The department's efforts are paying off. Clarke estimates that about one-quarter of her staff speaks a language other than English.

The Challenges of Implementing the Special Skills Classification

Clarke has had to exert strong leadership in supporting the special skills categories and the importance of cultural diversity within the department. When Clarke became the director in 1991, she received hate mail that claimed special skills workers were paid more than others for doing the same job and that non-special skills workers were being laid off first due to their race. Clarke sent a clear message that the hate mail was unacceptable and that attitudes needed to change. Clarke stood firm and disciplined employees when they harassed or discriminated against co-workers.

Other challenges arose over how to best use the special skills workers. Initially, a refugee bureau responsible for Indochinese clients was staffed entirely by Asian workers and supervisors. In time, Clarke came to believe that the bureau should be dispersed. First, she reasoned, this separate bureau meant that Asian clients had to come to one centralized location even though they lived throughout Sacramento. Second, Clarke was concerned that the bureau's mono-racial composition had drawbacks. An all-Asian unit meant that line-workers did not need to speak much English and could rely upon their supervisors to translate department rules and regulations. These language issues limited the extent to which staff could be transferred or promoted.

Nonetheless, dispersing the bureau was an extremely controversial process. The Asian workers suffered feelings of isolation and loneliness and faced significant harassment from co-workers who were racist or who resented the special status given to special skills workers.

As time passed, special skills workers also became concerned about how the category limited transfer opportunities. Initially, these employees kept their job classification during their entire tenure as a line worker. As a result, they could only be placed in offices where the demographics demonstrated a need for someone with their skills. Eventually, the department established a new policy. Special skills workers are now required to keep that classification for only two years. Then they can take a regular position, provided they are willing to lose the benefits associated with being a special skills worker.

County-Wide Reform: An Opportunity to Expand the Impact of Special Skills?

The special skills job classification has successfully created a large group of welfare workers capable of assisting linguistically and culturally diverse clients, but the impact on the overall department appears limited. The classifications affect only a portion of line workers and supervisors. They do not cover upper management and policy levels, which still fail to reflect the county's diversity. Also, the future of these job classifications remains unclear under the county's new system of human services.

In 1991, the Sacramento County Board of Supervisors moved to develop a more client-friendly, consumer-driven approach to providing services. The county reorganized its health and human services programs into three new departments: Human Assistance; Health and Human Services; and Medical Assistance. The Human Services Cabinet, which is the main body responsible for overseeing the reorganization and other interagency issues, includes representatives of key county, city, public and private agencies.

In addition, three demonstration sites have been created at the community level to test a new decentralized system of neighborhood service delivery. This system rests upon principles developed with substantial community input: strengthening individuals and preserving the family unit; assuring access to human services; emphasizing personal responsibility and self-sufficiency; and focusing on prevention. Fortunately, the special skills classification has made it easier for the county to find qualified, ethnically diverse staff for the pilot sites.

But questions remain. Under reorganization, the new Department of Health and Human Services was created from two sectors: nearly 600 workers from the original Health Department, combined with approximately 300 protective services workers formerly employed by the Welfare Department. The County is still pondering how to create a common set of personnel regulations for this new department. What happens to the special skills classification, which currently affects only the 300 protective services workers? Will it extend to all workers in Health and Human Services? Or will it be lost in the reorganization?

The profile of Sacramento illustrates that, particularly during this time of fiscal austerity, policy makers must carefully investigate the impact of seemingly race-neutral budget decisions concerning personnel. Layoffs according to seniority can disproportionately affect workers of color, however unintentional the result may be.

Sacramento is not the only community grappling with such issues. One school district we visited offered teachers early retirement in an effort to reduce costs. But the plan resulted in a significant reduction of African American teachers because a large majority of them were older. This loss has made it harder for schools to employ teachers who reflect the communities served.

Obviously, any decision to downsize personnel is difficult and requires balancing a number of important concerns. But it is critical for policymakers to thoroughly grasp beforehand all the different costs they are incurring, not just monetary ones. Policymakers could use such information to modify their plans and prevent disproportionate impact on a particular population. For example, the school district could have simultaneously offered incentives to stay for teachers who could demonstrate an ability to work with African American students, or it could have embarked upon a district-wide strategy to increase recruitment of African American teachers.

C. Re-Think How Services Are Financed

Funding can dictate the types of services provided, as well as the methods. The way the current system funds services plays a role in determining whether culturally and linguistically appropriate care becomes possible. For instance, some job requirements eliminate culturally competent candidates because programs can be reimbursed for a service only if it is performed by a worker with a specific credential. The current reform movement issues an important call to investigate how funding can better support the needs of clients rather than agencies.

Part of the attention should be directed at huge caseloads, which many providers feel inhibit their ability to take a client-centered, empowering approach to services. Most line staff in public agencies have caseloads that frequently number in the hundreds. Often, the social worker's job depends upon ability to demonstrate that s/he has processed a certain number of clients. Especially during recent layoffs and budget cuts, staff in many public agencies carry so many cases that they feel their jobs have been reduced to completing paperwork and verifying clients' eligibility for programs. There is no time to sit down with a family to ask members about their needs, much less develop a trusting relationship. Assessed on inputs (e.g. number of families processed or services provided) rather than client outcomes, systems are generally not set up to reward or even support staff who demonstrate that they can serve more effectively if they have fewer clients. Such conditions make it difficult to employ the strategies discussed in Chapter 3.

Some sites we visited addressed this problem by cutting the caseloads of staff members who were piloting new approaches to helping families. This strategy still has significant limitations, however. Typically, the public agencies redistributed the caseloads to other workers in the department. Often, this practice appeared to create resentment among workers and with the union, which perceived some workers obtaining better working conditions at the expense of other workers. To circumvent this problem, the Sacramento Department of Human Assistance finances reduced caseloads for outstationed social workers by asking partner agencies involved in collaborative pilot efforts (e.g. school districts) to cover the additional cost of hiring more staff to pick up the slack.

Policymakers must carefully investigate the impact of seemingly race-neutral budget decisions concerning personnel.

Drawing Strength from Diversity

These issues yield two questions worth further exploration: To what extent are reduced caseloads necessary for staff to implement more effective approaches to working with families? If smaller caseloads are essential, how can agencies create these conditions for greater numbers of workers?

Categorical funding also determines what types of services can be provided to which families. Typically, under this system, only certain services and supports are reimbursable. But in many cases, what a family needs, or what is culturally or linguistically appropriate, does not qualify. The following profile of San Francisco's Family Mosaic Project illustrates how concerns over funding led to an important new experiment aimed at fundamentally changing how services to children are financed.

PROFILE

Family Mosaic: Putting the Pieces Together in Partnership with Families

 Like his peers at other public agencies in San Francisco, psychologist Abner J. Boles III was frustrated with "the system." Boles, who works in the Division of Mental Health and Substance Abuse, shared a deepening sense that the fragmented system of mental health services was failing children and families.

For Boles, an African American, there was an even sharper awareness that current services were inadequate for children of color.(Of the families served by Family Mosaic, 87% are from communities of color). Even if an agency hired culturally and ethnically diverse staff to serve young people, these employees would still have to operate under the status quo, with no means to create more flexible or appropriate services. Said Boles: "It's difficult to provide culturally competent services if the only place you can put a kid is day treatment, if the only thing that they can do is take a kid out of a home."

*He and his colleagues knew that creating a more effective system of care for children with serious emotional problems and their families would require changing the way agencies did business. Radical restructuring had to happen. Not only did services need to become more flexible and culturally respon-*sive, but the system of funding that determined those services also needed fundamental change.

Such frustrations became the impetus for six public agencies in the city, ranging from the Department of Social Services to Community Mental Health, to join together to create the Family Mosaic project. With a four-year grant from the Robert Wood Johnson Foundation, Family Mosaic began serving families in December 1990.

Today, Family Mosaic clients receive services in a coherent, coordinated fashion. Services are flexible, family-focused, and culturally and linguistically appropriate. All staff who work with families receive training about culturally specific attitudes towards health care and services, and parents and children are asked what types of services are compatible with their background. In addition, because staff has found that traditional services are sometimes incompatible with the cultural values and traditions of clients, funds have been set aside for non-traditional services. For example, staff created a "shadow" service when it noticed that some children were not getting to school. Adults were hired as "shadows" to follow a youngster to school and ensure that s/he gets there on time.

These changes would have been impossible, except that ever since Family Mosaic began operating, it has steadily pursued development of a mechanism to provide for flexible funds. Currently, federal and state funding for services is categorical. Money is provided only for specified services and only to

Continued on page 70

---

clients who have fulfilled stringent eligibility guidelines. Thus, creating flexible and culturally appropriate services would require changing how services are funded.

Family Mosaic received an extra incentive to create a new funding mechanism from the Robert Wood Johnson Foundation, which wanted Family Mosaic to be more than a pilot project; the foundation was interested in having lasting impact on the service delivery system. It asked Family Mosaic to develop a long-term funding strategy to sustain the project beyond the four-year grant and provided the technical assistance to help develop a fiscal package.

As a result, Family Mosaic created a promising "capitation model." The capitation model differed from the traditional way mental health services are paid for. Under the capitation system, rather than agencies providing services and then billing the state for payment, agencies would receive payment from the state in advance.

The capitation model attracted the attention of the Special Projects Division in the State Department of Health Services. The state decided to give Family Mosaic a set amount per child — the capitated rate — and Family Mosaic would manage the money to provide an appropriate array of mental health services at a lower cost than under the current system. The capitation model met both the state's interest in reducing the cost of mental health services and Family Mosaic's desire to provide effective, appropriate and flexible care. The collaborative began its capitated payment mechanism in May 1993.

Boles believed all along that if service providers were not hampered by funding restrictions, they would do a better job: "We think that there is an inclination for service providers to want to do what is appropriate, what is effective, what is right. We felt that categorical funding predetermines services and agencies, makes it difficult for staff to operate that way, even a culturally sophisticated staff." Project Planner Joanna Uribe de Mena agreed that

"structural change doesn't come unless you change the way money flows and how money can be used and who controls it."

Considerable benefits have resulted. The flexible funding has freed staff members to use their imaginations to create a comprehensive array of services to 'wrap around' a family in order to respond to individual needs. According to Clinical Director Miriam Martinez, "We changed a lot to best meet the needs of the families."

After receiving a referral, staff work in multidisciplinary teams made up of Family Advocates and Family Workers to assess a child and create a plan of care that includes the comprehensive services and supports necessary to ensure better outcomes for that child. Referrals come from various sources: schools, juvenile probation, hospitals, private providers, residential treatment facilities, health, mental health, social services, legal services, parents/guardians/siblings, or the Family Mosaic Project itself. Before any plan can be implemented, the multidisciplinary team works with parents or guardians to negotiate a signed approval that the services are needed, wanted and appropriate.

The flexible funding also enables Family Mosaic to purchase culturally appropriate services from private providers and community-based agencies that have demonstrated effectiveness in serving ethnically diverse communities. This avenue increases access to services for families that would not go to a traditional agency for help, even agencies such as Family Mosaic, which is ethnically and linguistically diverse.

Now, Family Mosaic is working with three community-based, ethnically specific mental health agencies to develop a "mini-capitation" model. While the community-based organizations (CBOs) have to invest in creating the accounting and case management infrastructure for the mini-capitation, they will benefit in the long run. Project Planner Uribe de Mena said, "We say to these community-based organizations, 'This is a model we want to share with you; this is a model we all think is important to explore in order to be able to better control the design of services.'" But she added, with increasing emphasis on managed care, mini-capitation will enable the CBOs to become vendors to managed care entities that wish to purchase culturally appropriate mental health services. The CBOs will no longer be bound by old contract models. "You'll be developing your skills and capacities to do fee-for-service through this process," she tells the organizations.

However, the capitation and mini-capitation experiments also carry certain risks and challenges: First, the move to a fee-for-service system is a big change for community-based organizations, possibly requiring outside expertise and financing to build the necessary accounting and case management software infrastructure. Second, projecting actual costs and utilization of services in the first year of the capitation plan is tricky. Because San Francisco requires contracts for set amounts with community-based organizations, Family Mosaic has to "guess-timate" and set aside funds. If it guesses high and sets aside too much, funds are tied up and can't be used for other services. If it guesses low, community-based organizations may not get their money quickly. Third, Family Mosaic needs to do outreach to develop a larger provider pool. Fourth, documenting the cost savings and tracking outcomes will be crucial. Last, because Family Mosaic serves only the "high end" users — children and families who have not been helped through other systems — cost overruns are a potential difficulty. (However, the capitated rate is renegotiable).

The challenges are certainly great, but one evaluation already indicates that this new way of serving families is having a positive impact on severely emotionally disturbed children. Using five indicators of better functioning (increased school attendance; improved school performance; decreased rates of psychiatric hospitalization; decreased rates of incarceration; and increased family participation), Family Mosaic found significant improvements for the 175 children who had received services.

Family Mosaic's capitation model is one example of how financing mechanisms can be created to make services more responsive and appropriate for communities, while simultaneously achieving lower cost for services.

· ·

A crucial element of the Family Mosaic strategy is the use of the "mini-capitation" model as an attempt to strengthen and support community-based organizations. Typically located in the neighborhoods where client families reside, CBOs traditionally have extensive experience in providing culturally and linguistically appropriate services. Partly because they are not subject to the rigid credentialing requirements that confine public agencies, CBOs are more likely to employ bilingual staff who also live in the community.

While it is true, as in any field, that some CBOs have ceased to work for the best interests of the community, CBOs in general remain an invaluable source of knowledge and expertise. One challenge is to discover how funding in a reformed system of services can be used to increase the capacity of CBOs to provide needed services *and* work in close collaboration with public agencies.

As the services reform movement grows, it is also important to keep in mind that proposed changes to current funding methods are not always viewed positively, particularly by community-based organizations. For example, the growing focus on interagency collaboration has led many funders, public and private, to require agencies to collaborate in order to receive a grant. In many ways, this new requirement is a drastic departure from the way many CBOs have learned to obtain funding, particularly from public sources. Many CBOs, originally established to serve a population within a particular geographic area, have

Collaboration among community-based organizations can help to ensure that diverse families have access to services.

learned to obtain funding by competing with each other and by working the political network. Established non-profits often resist collaboration because they have developed the power to wield resources. Knowing that funding decisions are often based on politics as much as on the merits of a proposal, non-profits ensure support for funding requests by registering voters and seeking the election and appointment of key officials from their communities. Collaborative funding requirements not only change how CBOs go about obtaining resources, but may also compel them to work with the very groups which they competed against for influence over the political process.

Some CBOs, particularly those in minority communities, have viewed the shift in funding as yet another example of people in power changing the rules of the game just as they learned how the play by the rules of the previous system.

The intent of this discussion is not to suggest that funders are wrong to encourage inter-agency collaboration as a means to improve services for children and families. Rather, the discourse illustrates the importance of engaging affected CBOs in discussions about why collaboration is necessary, then providing them with technical assistance and support to meet the new funding requirements. Safeguards are needed to prevent effective organizations from accidentally being forced out of business because they lacked the administrative capacity to adapt to a changing environment.

In a world where demographics are changing rapidly, collaboration among community-based organizations can help to ensure that diverse families have access to services. CBOs can reap tremendous benefits as they tap into each other's organizational strengths and expertise in working with particular populations. One consultant we interviewed told how he helped facilitate such a relationship. One community, as a whole, was struggling to meet the needs of incoming refugees from Southeast Asia. The established organization with the most developed organizational capacity and the lion's share of funding targeted at Asians was staffed by ethnic Chinese whose families had lived in the United States for several generations. In contrast, the newer groups working with refugees were relatively unsophisticated and had far fewer contacts with funding sources. Though the process was not easy, the Chinese organization and the newer groups formed a consortium to "capture" new monies targeted at refugees. The consortium was formed with the understanding that the Chinese organization would serve initially as the lead agency and would be responsible for training personnel from the refugee groups in organizational administration. After two years, the lead agency status shifted over to the refugee community.

D. Use Outcomes Accountability and
Reflective Practice to Increase Attention to Diversity

Ultimately, truly addressing diversity at the institutional level requires creation of a system by which service providers continually evaluate whether their policies and practices are supporting the healthy development of all children and families. Furthermore, service providers must assess whether they are having positive impact on constantly changing communities.

In California, the pace of change is dizzying. Neighborhoods formerly populated by one dominant group are now a mix of peoples — groups with different family structures and languages. The strategies that support one population may not work for another, or may even have detrimental results. Laurie Olsen, co-director of California Tomorrow, states:

"Vigilance requires that we ask hard questions of ourselves and our practice. Vigilance requires that we gather the data which can tell us where our institutions are lapsing into patterns of exclusion, denial or differential impact."

Holding programs responsible for outcomes achieved — not simply inputs (e.g. the number of families served or the types of services provided) — is one institutional change being advocated by the reform movement which could compel agencies to pay much closer attention to how well they are working with diverse populations. At this time, very few agencies are ever held accountable in any fashion for the results they produce.

This shift toward outcomes-based accountability is occurring for a number of reasons. First, this new system offers hope of freeing professionals from the micro-management that constrains their ability to respond flexibly, appropriately and creatively to the needs of each family. Judged by whether or not they achieve a particular outcome rather than how they provided a service, professionals would be able to modify plans and draw upon family and community strengths. Outcomes-based accountability could present a positive alternative to the restrictions of categorical funding discussed in the Family Mosaic profile. It could also ensure that scarce resources are used wisely on programs and strategies that can prove their effectiveness. Over time, such evidence of efficient use of tax dollars could increase public confidence in government programs.

It is important, however, to keep in mind that agencies and advocates view outcomes-based accountability with mixed reactions. Some support the idea, but others fear that outcomes measurement will be misused as a cover for further funding cutbacks. Or, as author Lisbeth B. Schorr writes, "outcomes accountability will be used to penalize individual professionals, institutions, and agencies who may not be achieving hoped-for results, but are trying hard and doing the best they can."

History and diversity contribute to the ambivalence over outcomes accountability. Traditionally, certain strategies have been used to assure services to populations that have faced discrimination. For instance, advocates in the field of education have often used categorical funding and restrictions on agency discretion to ensure that resources are spent on historically underserved populations. Federal Chapter One funding, for example, is set aside only for underachieving, low-income students in schools with large numbers of poor children. Many advocates, who have fought long, hard battles to obtain these categorical funding streams, are wary when discussions about outcomes accountability arise because they fear an erosion of protections for traditionally underserved students.

In contrast, some categorical restrictions are not the products of advocacy efforts, but are administrative attempts to control costs. For example, Aid to Families with Dependent Children (AFDC) eligibility requirements are designed to protect the government from spending money on individuals not truly in need of aid. In other programs, regulations control costs by allowing for reimbursement of only certain types of services and support.

Nevertheless, policymakers and practitioners can take steps to address fears that the shift to outcomes accountability will erode crucial protections. Certain measures can also be taken to assure that outcomes accountability will result in greater attention to issues of diversity. These involve: 1) using data broken down by relevant categories (e.g. race, gender, language background) to engage diverse groups in examining how agency practices might need to change in order to serve diverse populations more effectively, 2) creating opportunities for diverse stakeholders to define the outcomes to which institutions and programs should be held accountable, and 3) embedding these principles in program evaluation.

1. Use Disaggregated Data to Examine Agency Practice

Data broken down (or disaggregated) by the categories most relevant for a particular community (e.g. race/ethnicity, language, gender, income, geographic area, age) provides critical information about a program's effectiveness in serving diverse populations equitably and appropriately. Such information can shed light on whether groups are under- or over-utilizing services, whether interventions are resulting in equally good results for all families, or whether an agency is intentionally or unintentionally engaging in discriminatory practices. Examining disaggregated data offers one strategy for using outcomes to maintain protections for historically underserved populations.

Are interventions resulting in equally good results for all families?

To fully understand the implications of disaggregated data, it is important to draw upon diverse perspectives for analysis. For example, at one site we visited, planners wondered why the proportion of African American families living in the housing project was significantly lower than the proportion of African American families eligible to live there. The eligibility requirements were based solely on income and therefore, race-neutral. After probing, planners found that African American families were evicted at a much higher rate than other families. This revelation sparked a hot debate among collaborative members. Was the disproportionate eviction rate due to the behavior of African American families? Or was it due to some systemic factors? Some argued that African American families tended to be louder or more likely to be engaged in criminal activity, such as drug dealing; therefore, they should be evicted because such activities violated lease terms. Others argued that the housing authority focused on African American families and failed to look at other families, for instance Asians, who were perceived to be less troublesome, although they were similarly engaged in criminal activity. The interpretations of these data have forced a deeper discussion of what constitutes success for this community. Is success achieved when all troublemakers are evicted? Or does something more profound need to occur among families in the complex? Figuring out an appropriate response ultimately will require asking Asian and African American residents how they feel about the evictions.

While this example demonstrates how disaggregated data can be used to detect problems with agency practices, it is also important to remember that such data can be used to evaluate the effectiveness of new approaches to working with families. In this case, outcomes accountability can offer groups a chance to prove that culturally and linguistically appropriate services are instrumental to improving outcomes for children and families.

Persuading agencies to use disaggregated data requires sensitivity to the issues involved in examining this type of information. Many agencies avoid looking at such data because they fear the data will be used to penalize them, despite the fact that they are working hard to improve conditions for children and families. Tying funding to outcomes also has the potential to create a disincentive to collecting disaggregated data. Fearing that immediate job losses or program dissolution will result, service providers may be inclined to collect only data that justify continuation of funding and not report their failures.

Fears about data collection can be intensified when programs are required to look at data disaggregated by race or language group. Some providers may fear how communities they serve will react to this information. Others may fear that the data will be misused to blame particular racial or ethnic groups for their problems rather than be used to monitor the system for failing to achieve equitable outcomes.

Forming an environment that encourages collaboratives to take a hard look at data requires creating a system of accountability in which organizations are given a chance to make changes before they are threatened with loss of funding. It also involves providing collaboratives with supports and technical assistance on how to use and interpret data, as well as to engage diverse groups in discussing beneficial changes. While such support is essential, it is also important to understand that in some cases, funding should be taken from an agency so that it can be given to another that can do a better job. Outcomes accountability can help detect which agencies are best equipped to meet the needs of particular populations. Such agencies should be rewarded for their positive results with additional funds.

2. Involve Diverse Stakeholders in Establishing Outcomes

Diverse perspectives are critical to interpreting the implications of disaggregated data, but multiple viewpoints are also integral to establishing the outcomes to which programs should be held accountable. Sometimes groups oppose outcomes accountability for fear that those who control major financial resources will set the outcomes exclusively, and that these outcomes will not be realistic, achievable or appropriate. First, engaging the perspectives of diverse stakeholders (youth, parents, service providers, and program administrators) is critical to ensuring that outcomes are achievable and realistic, given the available resources, and that outcomes are suitable to community needs. Second, involving these key stakeholders in setting outcomes helps to ensure that they buy into the process and therefore are willing to implement new strategies. The history of social services reform is filled with change efforts that failed by neglecting to involve and gain the support of the very individuals responsible for carrying them out.

Cultural and racial experience can have a significant impact in shaping what a person believes is an appropriate outcome.

Issues of cultural and linguistic diversity make an inclusive process even more important because cultural and racial experience can have a significant impact in shaping what a person believes is an appropriate outcome. Engaging culturally diverse perspectives is critical to determining what types of outcomes would be reasonable goals for all program participants, regardless of ethnicity, and whether the program may need to allow for some differences by ethnic group.

Consider, for instance, how a program that addresses teen pregnancy could engender differing ideas of desirable outcomes among groups. Middle-class white parents might believe that the most appropriate outcome is a reduction in the rate of teen pregnancy. But this goal could seem unreasonable to another ethnic group that encourages women to marry and bear children at a young age. Both groups, however, are likely to agree that the program should increase teenagers' understanding of the responsibilities and lifestyle changes that accompany parenthood. The program might then decide to look at several different outcomes: how well participants understand the responsibilities of parenthood; the rate of teen-age pregnancy; and the degree to which teens with children demonstrate that they are good parents. Positive results in any of these areas could then be used as indicators of success.

Involving diverse stakeholders in setting outcomes also sends an important message about power. Often, the individuals who control resources belong to a different class and/or racial background than those who receive services. If program participants are not involved in setting outcomes, they may be highly suspicious of the program and its motives.

3. Embed These Principles in Program Evaluation

Taking the steps described above — using data broken down by relevant categories and involving diverse stakeholders in defining outcomes — has direct implications for program evaluation and the role of evaluators.

First, evaluators should incorporate an analysis of data broken down by relevant categories — such as race/ethnicity, language, gender, income, geographic area, or age — into any evaluation of a program. The evaluator can also play an important role in helping program staff and administrators to present this information to the community in easily understood forms.

Evaluators need to work closely with stakeholders, such as community residents and agency line staff, to define measurable goals and outcomes.

Second, evaluators need to work closely with stakeholders, such as community residents and agency line staff, to define measurable goals and outcomes. This implies that evaluators should get involved with programs early on, ideally as part of the community assessment process. According to experienced evaluators Brindis, Philliber, and Kaplan, "needs assessment and program evaluation should be considered as parts of a continuum of programmatic efforts aimed at increasing the effectiveness of services and supports." If evaluators are not involved in the early stages of program development, they risk assessing a program for outcomes that differ from those defined by the community. Evaluators who work closely with community residents and agency staff also challenge traditional assumptions that the best evaluator maintains distance from a program to prevent tainting the evaluation through personal knowledge of program participants.

Working with community residents and agency staff requires evaluators to exercise more than just technical skills. They also must be able to build trust with ethnically and linguistically diverse communities, communicate effectively, and resolve disparate views of desired outcomes. One evaluator who has worked on several integrated services initiatives described the broader process skills that working with diverse stakeholders has required of her:

> "Evaluators are trained primarily in the technology of evaluation. We learn to 'crunch numbers.' Sometimes we also learn qualitative skills. But we don't learn to deal with the process, that is, the understanding and skills needed to work in complex, fluid situations where human beings are trying to understand and change their reality. This calls for a whole different set of skills, ones with which those trained in traditional social sciences are often neither familiar nor particularly comfortable."

Evaluators must also have the patience to allow community residents to generate their own outcomes, rather than impose personal preferences or funders' preferences upon stakeholders. Similarly, evaluators must ensure that agencies identify the kind of feedback they need, and that agencies also have the ongoing capacity to define outcomes and hold themselves accountable for results.

The third implication is that evaluators become accountable to all stakeholders, not only to the funder. This often creates tensions for the evaluator as s/he tries to balance her/his ethical responsibilities to different groups. Evaluator Zoe Clayson explains:

> "When you are an evaluator, there are all these accountabilities. Normally, the evaluator thinks that they are just accountable to the person who is giving the money, who signs your paycheck. But the question remains: Are you accountable to the funder, the program itself, or the relationship to the community? Are you accountable to the individual or the family?"

Evaluators seeking to balance responsibilities to these different groups face some real dilemmas. On one hand, they are encouraging program staff to identify where their efforts are not successful in order to take corrective action. On the other hand, sharing such information with funders, who base future funding decisions on evidence of program effectiveness, could violate program staff's trust in the evaluator and possibly lead to loss of funding. In order for evaluators to resolve such dilemmas, funders must be willing to step outside their traditional roles and be willing to support different types of evaluations. Says evaluator Claire Brindis:

> "The traditional mode of evaluation has been, 'If you don't do well, or if the evaluation shows that you haven't done a good job, we're going to take your funding away.' A few innovative funders have taken a different approach. They understand that these are demonstration-type programs. They understand the need to build the capacity of programs themselves to learn what works, as well as what did not work. They see the importance of giving programs time to identify and remedy problems and not simply use evaluations to make funding decisions."

Evaluators on the cutting edge of program evaluation in diverse communities continue to grapple with questions of professional ethics and responsibility. Answers are still emerging. These are important issues that require further attention from funders, research institutions and training programs in universities.

Evaluators become accountable to all stakeholders, not only to the funder.

CHAPTER 6

Who Makes Decisions?

Involving the Community in Governance

People in a democratic society have a right to shape the direction of policies and services that affect their lives.

Another common theme of human services reform efforts is a growing emphasis on including community members in decision-making and governance. This chapter describes why policymakers are moving toward community governance and the extent to which initiatives currently involve diverse stakeholders. We found that public agencies and community-based organizations were involved in the overwhelming majority of the surveyed collaborative programs. Individuals who can add the perspectives of the diverse communities served are, however, still largely missing.

These results reflect the fact that implementing the concept of community governance can be an extremely difficult proposition. The rest of this chapter explores challenges facing the field and some strategies which groups have developed in response. We also feature a profile of the Vaughn Family Center, an innovative effort to engage a community in governance, and a profile of the San Diego New Beginnings program.

A. The Movement Toward Community Governance

As a beginning measure, many human services reform initiatives have brought together the agencies that serve families. This focus on interagency collaboration stems from the recognition that no agency alone has the resources or the knowledge to fully meet the needs of families. Over time, however, an increasing number of groups have become aware that this focus on agencies is not enough. Instead of paying attention only to agencies and services, some collaborative efforts have begun to see the importance of promoting self-sufficiency and community governance. (See the accompanying New Beginnings profile on page 91)

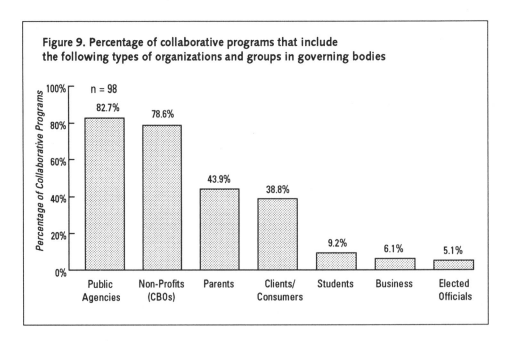

Figure 9. Percentage of collaborative programs that include the following types of organizations and groups in governing bodies

The emphasis on bringing the community into decision-making circles has evolved for many reasons. First, it reflects a fundamental American belief that people in a democratic society have a right to shape the direction of policies and services that affect their lives. Decisions have greater legitimacy when they are made by a group that reflects the community. Second, involving community members in governance is seen as a means for ensuring accountability to the community being served. Third, it helps to ensure a group encompasses the range of perspectives critical to helping it understand appropriate versus inappropriate strategies for working with the families and children served. Last, community participation in governance endows people with a sense of dignity and charges them with responsibility for solving their own problems. It removes the sense of dependence and passivity that comes from being on the receiving end of assistance.

B. The Extent to which Governance Structures Reflect Communities

To explore the make-up of decision-making bodies, California Tomorrow surveyed collaboratives to find out what types of groups and individuals participated in making policy and program decisions. It is important to note, however, that answering questions about governance is not always easy for collaboratives. Collaboration is a developmental process. In the initial stages, participants typically participate on a more informal basis. They share information and attend meetings but may not have formally designated decision-making responsibilities. Because participants may not attend meetings on a regular basis, collaboratives often have difficulty identifying exactly who is involved in governance. As collaboratives become more developed, decision-making processes and responsibilities become clearer. Functions of formal governance structures can include determining the allocation of resources, hiring staff, and being held accountable for results. One of the limitations of our survey is it did not allow us to assess the extent to which governance had been formalized by the collaborative. Nonetheless, survey responses offered useful information about the types of groups involved in shaping the scope and direction of collaborative initiatives. Our data suggest collaboratives have been able to involve a broad array of service providers, but still struggle to include community representatives.

Service Providers: Not surprisingly, given the emphasis on interagency collaboration, public agencies and non-profit community-based organizations were usually represented. Of the 98 collaboratives surveyed, 82.7% have public agencies on their governing bodies and 78.6% include community-based organizations. A handful included representatives from the business community or elected officials.

Community Perspectives: Our survey looked for the presence of people who reflect the diverse perspectives within a community in two ways. One approach was to ask about the general presence of consumer and community perspectives — parents, clients, and students. These groups were missing in the majority of collaboratives. Only 38.8% of the collaboratives had clients on the governing bodies, 43.9% included parents and a mere 9.2% had students. (See Figure 9)

In addition, we used survey responses about the racial background of their board members to assess the extent to which collaboratives included representatives from the communities being served. If a collaborative indicated that it served a particular racial group,

Community participation in governance endows people with a sense of dignity and charges them with responsibility for solving their own problems.

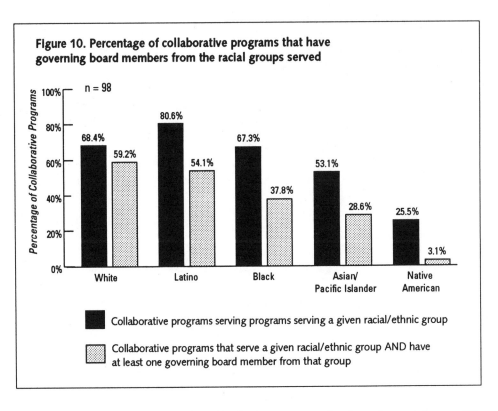

Figure 10. Percentage of collaborative programs that have governing board members from the racial groups served

n = 98

Percentage of Collaborative Programs

White: 68.4% / 59.2%
Latino: 80.6% / 54.1%
Black: 67.3% / 37.8%
Asian/Pacific Islander: 53.1% / 28.6%
Native American: 25.5% / 3.1%

■ Collaborative programs serving programs serving a given racial/ethnic group

▦ Collaborative programs that serve a given racial/ethnic group AND have at least one governing board member from that group

we checked whether its governing board had at least one member from that racial group. We found that a significant number of collaboratives did not have at least one board member from one or more of the racial groups being served. The lack of reflectiveness is most serious for Native Americans and Asian/Pacific Islanders. Only 3.1% of the collaboratives in our sample reported having a Native American on the governing body although 25.5% of the programs serve Native Americans. And only 28.6% have an Asian/Pacific Islander on their governing body although 53.1% serve Asian/Pacific Islanders. (See Figure 10)

We believe these data underestimate the extent of the problem because of the limitations of our methodology. As discussed in the staffing chapter, race is only a general indicator of whether a person is able to represent the interests of the community. As the earlier discussion on staffing suggests, a number of factors (e.g. race, class, or place of residence) also have an impact on the ability of a person to provide insights into the issues facing a community. A single racial category also encompasses a number of ethnic categories. Anecdotal information from our interviews and site visits suggests that collaboratives would be even less representative if these other considerations could have been taken into account. In addition, the criterion we used — the presence of a single board member — is a minimal requirement. We used this criterion because the complete absence of a person of the same racial background as the programs' clientele seemed to be a clear indication of the lack of a particular group's perspective. But, just having a single individual from a particular group on a board does not ensure his or her voice has an impact. A sole representative of a particular group can easily feel both isolated and marginalized. It is also important to note that a small number of survey participants refused to answer the questions at all. Their written explanations suggested they were indignant that we even asked questions about racial background.

Drawing Strength from Diversity

C. Creating Meaningful Community Governance: Challenges and Strategies

The results of our collaborative survey are not surprising given the challenging nature of engaging in community governance. Collaboratives involved in creating a governance body that includes large public agencies and community-based organizations already know how difficult it is to work together given the differences in organizational missions, agency cultures and languages, disciplinary perspectives, and historical rivalries. Including representation from the various ethnic communities served adds another layer of complexity. It is just as difficult, if not more difficult to work across differences of culture and language. The following section explores challenges faced by reform initiatives. Where possible, material describing strategies used by groups to respond to these challenges is also offered. Information on strategies, however, is still limited. Clearly groups are still grappling with how to implement the concept of community governance.

1. Taking the Community's Size and Scope into Account

Community governance can be difficult to achieve when the "community" itself encompasses extremely diverse interests and lacks a sense of cohesiveness. The size and nature of the community served makes a tremendous difference. For example, community governance may be easier to achieve at a housing project where residents are consolidated into a small, defined geographic area, have more opportunities to know their neighbors and collaborative staff, and have experience working together in groups such as tenants' associations.

Establishing a community governance structure may be much more difficult with larger communities such as a county. Unlike a housing project, there are many more people living in a county. They are widely dispersed and various ethnic groups may not know one another. These are all factors that make community governance more difficult to achieve.

2. Bridging Cultural and Linguistic Barriers

Many collaboratives find they are unable to involve key stakeholders from a particular ethnic group because they do not understand the culture or the language well enough to develop strategies for encouraging their participation. Organizers may not even realize that the tactics they are using to reach out to new groups are inappropriate and sometimes even alienating.

In these types of situations, community-based organizations (CBOs) can be a critical source of help. Often, CBOs are centrally located in neighborhoods and have culturally specific services and bilingual staff. As a result, CBOs frequently have a better understanding of and relationship to specific ethnic communities than public agencies. Including CBOs in the collaboration helps to ensure access to their knowledge about the most effective strategies and approaches for involving particular populations.

Members of particular ethnic groups may also offer crucial insights. In one community, building bridges to a hard-to-reach group of parents was a simple matter of asking people from that ethnic community what approach would be most effective. The following story illustrates this point.

The Real Significance
of Making Cupcakes

In recent years, Yuba County California has seen a dramatic influx of Hmong families from Southeast Asia. Hired as CIA military operatives during the Vietnam War, the Hmong were forced to flee as political refugees when the United States lost the war. Although the U.S. government guaranteed them immigration to this country, many Hmong lost their lives or family members during traumatic escapes. Now that the journey is over, the Hmong face the almost inconceivable challenge of moving from a largely agrarian, pre-literate society in the Laotian highlands to modern America in a single lifetime.

A major part of the Yuba County Coordinated Services Project is the development of school-linked services at two elementary schools that have large numbers of Hmong children enrolled. When these efforts began, the planning group was at a loss about how to involve Hmong families. Few Hmong parents ever showed up for school events, despite efforts to send notes and telephone them.

Finally, one woman from the planning group decided to pay home visits, accompanied by two Hmong translators. She asked one parent what activity would make it worthwhile to come to a meeting at school. The parent's answer: "We would like to learn to make cupcakes."

All too often, Hmong parents had been asked by their children to make cupcakes for a school event or social activity, but had to disappoint them because they did not know what a cupcake was. The next meeting included a cupcake-making session, and the planning group was overwhelmed by the parents' attendance and enthusiasm. Since that breakthrough, Hmong mothers and fathers have slowly but surely become more comfortable with coming to the school and playing an increasingly active role.

. . . .

3. Encouraging the Participation of the Least Enfranchised

Simply opening decision-making processes to include community people does not ensure the participation of groups most affected by the initiative — those who will receive services. When such groups are not represented, their concerns may be overlooked. At worst, decisions may have negative impacts on these groups.

For example, one pilot project in Sacramento County has attempted to engage community members in governing an initiative aimed at providing neighborhood-based heath and social services. When the project began seeking the participation of community members, the first group to show up at meeting were leaders from among the established African-American home owners and local small businesses. Reaching out to the recently arrived Tongan and Southeast Asian communities has proven much more challenging. Contact with these new groups has been inhibited by language barriers and a lack of established community-based organizations with strong relations to these new populations. The largely middle-class and business-dominated community representatives generally oppose providing services because they fear they will draw low-income renters into the area. Staff at the pilot project believe, however, these are exactly the sorts of services the Tongans and Southeast Asians need.

In another community that attempted to provide primary health services in elementary schools, program implementation was almost stopped because fundamentalist Christian groups began campaigning against the proposed initiative. The fundamentalist groups felt it was a first step towards getting school involved in family planning. From the beginning, however, the founders of the program had sought and fostered the active participation of the group most affected: Latino parents with children in the schools. When the project was brought to the school board for approval, the poignant testimonies of Latino mothers about the need for services was instrumental in making sure the board understood the project was supported by the majority of the community.

Actively promoting leadership development — so that all groups (particularly, parents, youth and other client populations) feel empowered to make decisions about programs and services which affect their lives — is critical. There is clearly a need for additional research and development in this area of building community capacity and leadership. What are the skills required by community residents? Which groups can work effectively with community residents to foster these skills? The answers are still emerging. What we do know is that some research demonstrates that activities aimed at empowerment can result in "increased self-esteem and assertiveness, greater feelings of control over life circumstances, increased sense of attachment and belonging and a growing conviction that one is making a contribution to the larger whole."[1] The Razalogia program adopted by the Family Resource Schools in Denver, Colorado illustrates the approach taken by one initiative.

The Razalogia
Parent Empowerment Program

"¡Sí se puede!"— or "Yes, I can!"— has become the attitude adopted by many Latino mothers and fathers engaged in Razalogia, a parent empowerment and education program in Denver schools. Razalogia's motto reflects its mission: to build parents' confidence and abilities so that they will become involved in their children's education, participate in decision-making, and take leadership positions in schools.

The Razalogia model was designed with Latino parents in mind, but is relevant for parents of any background. Since 1988, the Razalogia empowerment philosophy has been a guiding light at Denver's Family Resource Schools, which go beyond the traditional role of public elementary schools by providing students and their families with health and human services. These special campuses place strong emphasis on working in partnership with parents.

Continued on page 84

---

[1]Cochran, "Parent Empowerment: Developing a Conceptual Framework," Family Science Review, Vol. 5, No. 1 & 2, Feb. & May 1992.

Many parents remark that Razalogia, which undergirds all parent programs, has helped build their self-esteem and confidence. For Jennifer Chavez, who initially came to get help with being a battered wife, "parenting classes helped me get my self-esteem back." Another mother, Jessica Lopez, said she has learned to talk more confidently to people:

"Razalogia has done a lot for me. I had a big issue with my daughter's teacher. I didn't know how to go about this problem. This parenting class gave me the courage. It taught me how to confront my child's teacher without getting all mad and angry."

Now Lopez volunteers at her child's school for several hours each day. She also recruits other parents to become involved in Razalogia by telling them, "a simple person like us can get the education and knowledge we need."

Several tenets anchor Razalogia, which means "the study of our race." The main premise is that to gain power, parents must have knowledge; all people can learn from their life experiences. "Educare" means to draw from within oneself for answers. But "dialogue," or speaking with others, also helps parents to solve problems. The concept of "transformative consciousness" is defined as one's inner motivation to work for change. "Praxis" means that nothing changes unless you put what you know into practice.

Community bonding among parents promotes mutual understanding. Through Razalogia, the parents — predominantly Mexican — are taught about cultural conflict. They identify the values that Mexicans bring with them, then discuss general American values. Parents learn to recognize and deal with conflict. They are taught that the solution is not to give up their home values, but to know when to embrace an American value as well. Razalogia emphasizes respect for one another's values. It explains the concept of diversity with the metaphor, "We are all flowers from the same garden."

As self-confidence has grown, many parents have taken roles in school activities and learned enough about how the schools function to be able to participate in governance, specifically the Collaborative Decision-Making (commonly known as "CDM") bodies which have been established in all Denver schools. The CDMs give parents a voice in educational design and other school-related matters, thereby promoting a sense of parent and community ownership and partnership with the schools. CDM bodies at school sites generally consist of equal numbers of teachers and parents, the principal, the family resource coordinator, and two classified staff. CDMs are responsible for hiring, personnel issues, building linkages between the school and the community, and have final "write-off" on instructional programming. All members, except the principal and family resource coordinator, are elected to two-year terms by their peer groups.

Jennifer Chavez, the mother who first came to Cheltenham Elementary for help with spousal abuse, was elected to a two-year term on the school's CDM committee. She said her other role as president of Cheltenham's Bilingual Program Advisory

Committee has already shown her children "that I can do it. I always have been a good mother, but now my children see me being involved in the community." Participating at school has been a growing experience, she says:

> "I've come a long way in the last three years — from nothing to somebody. I was chosen to be a model parent on a TV show. It's a wonderful feeling for me and my kids to have gotten so far in life. I want to show my children it can be done. They don't need to wait until they are thirty years old."

• •

While Razalogia is aimed at parents, programs can also take steps to develop the skills and leadership potential of the youth involved in their programs. The Casa Loma Torch Club, described in Chapter 2, teaches democratic traditions to youths and calls upon them to perform community services. At San Francisco's Everett Middle School, also profiled in Chapter 2, students had the opportunity to assess needs at their school and then advocate for changes.

4. Addressing the Legacy of Token Governance

Community governance is not a new concept; many people, especially minorities, are wary of participating in yet another token effort in which their presence is used to lend legitimacy and credibility to an initiative, but their voice has no impact. Individuals or groups who have had such experiences may be understandably reluctant to participate. Feelings of tokenism can result from different situations. In some cases, community members become jaded when they discover that they have much less decision-making authority than they were initially led to believe. They realize, for example, that the group's decisions are considered advisory rather than binding. Or, they find that they are unable to wield enough power to affect decision-making processes because they always constitute a political minority within a larger governance structure. As a result, their voices and ideals are defeated consistently.

Some communities become disillusioned because an inclusive process of decision-making is not respected. Consider what frequently unfolds when a funder offers a grant, provided that a community delivers a proposal by a certain deadline. This type of situation often puts leaders of a community process in a bind. On one hand, they want to move quickly so that they don't lose the money. On the other hand, democratic processes can be slow and unwieldy; they often do not lend themselves to quick decisions. But making a unilateral decision can be more detrimental in the long run because it breeds distrust in the process, and the proposal's strategies fail to build upon the knowledge of the community. Groups faced with this situation must carefully weigh the costs and benefits.

5. Dealing with Group Power Dynamics

Participation can also be inhibited by real differences in power and knowledge. Often, individuals who hold greater power and authority may unwittingly intimidate those with less power in a room. One consultant noted how differences in class background and knowledge gained from experience actually inhibit participation during collaborative meetings:

When the newcomers are of a different class or speak different languages than the older residents, communication and understanding are difficult. It may be very common for middle-class professionals to look over a budget. They tend to do that a lot; they know how that all works. If you have not been on a board before, and someone hands you a budget with all these income and expense categories, are you going to sit there and ask a series of questions in front of everyone to expose your ignorance? Most people won't.

In an diverse setting it is easy for someone to feel alienated, especially if a person is the sole representative of his or her group. Some may feel uncomfortable with attending meetings or dislike the way meetings are conducted. Others might feel that their views are discounted.

Encouraging equal participation in the decision-making process requires a conscious effort.

Encouraging equal participation in the decision-making process requires a conscious effort. One strategy to address differences in knowledge and power is to create opportunities before and after governance meetings, for newcomers to ask questions in private, comfortable settings. Another strategy, as described in the profile of the Vaughn Family Center on page 87, is to have role plays before meetings to orient new members on procedures.

Strong meeting facilitation can also help to address some of these dynamics. Two common principles we have seen employed are: take the time to build trust and establish ground rules. Whenever diverse groups of people come together to make decisions that will affect the livelihoods of their families and communities, they must have time to develop trust, respect and relationships if they hope to work together. They also must understand each other's perspectives and agendas so that they can see their common hopes and objectives as well as respect their differences. Some of this understanding can be fostered by creating opportunities for people to talk to each other about their values, beliefs and personal experiences, particularly if they do not know each other well. Another approach is to establish committees where people work on a common task in multiethnic teams. Trust-building often evolves from the simple act of laboring together over a period of time.

Ground rules are essential to promoting clarity and understanding in any setting. They are particularly important when a group is diverse. Consider the importance of discussing and defining what the groups agrees is an indication of consensus. Even in a group that shares a common culture, consensus can be unclear. When a show of hands or verbal vote is taken, a "yes" vote can mean several things: total endorsement of the proposal, agreement with reservations or the lack of opposition without any commitment to take responsibility for implementation. Misunderstandings about consensus are compounded in an ethnically diverse group because cultural expressions of consensus may differ. For example, in some cultures, silence can mean discussion is finished and consensus has been reached. In other cultures, silence may signal lack of agreement. Similarly, a ground rule about respecting differences of opinion can be critical to fostering an atmosphere of open dialogue. Disagreements are bound to arise in any groups, particularly if the participants come from different perspectives. Some people feel uncomfortable with dissension because they have been raised to believe that open disagreement is problematic. Without a ground rule, they may take action to quell discussion when conflicting opinions appear to be arising. In diverse groups, however, being able to openly discussing disagreements and why they exist is essential to making better decisions.

Despite the challenges inherent to community governance, it is important to keep in mind that some groups have moved effectively in this direction. The following profile illustrates how one collaborative services initiative used various strategies to create a governance structure that reflects the communities served.

The Vaughn Family Center

Nestled in a low-income Pacoima neighborhood in the heart of the San Fernando Valley is the Vaughn Next Century Learning Center, a public elementary school. Its students are mostly Latinos, with a small population of African Americans. A large proportion of families are living in poverty or have recently immigrated.

To serve these households, the school houses the Vaughn Family Center, which collaborates with various agencies to provide comprehensive health, educational and social services. These offerings include dental care, immunizations, housing assistance, tutoring, counseling, aerobics, English classes, legal aid, and parent leadership development, to name a few.

In many ways, the Vaughn Family Center is similar to other integrated services initiatives. But it is distinguished by one of its unique and powerful components: the high degree of parent participation in every aspect of the project, including governance.

On any given day, the Family Center bustles with activity. One can observe children reading or working on art projects as they are being cared for by parent volunteers. Often, parents will meet in the center to discuss issues of concern or to prepare for a school potluck.

A 40-member commission of equal numbers of parents and service providers oversees the project. This commission makes decisions on the hiring of center staff and the types of services provided. Such a governing structure allows parents equal voice in shaping the services delivered to them and also helps build their capacity to understand their own strengths and resources.

Parents at the Vaughn Family Center

The Vaughn Center is the first demonstration site of the Family Care collaboration launched by the Los Angeles Educational Partnership and the North Angeles Region of United Way. The initiative is funded primarily by foundation and private corporation donations and a SB620 Healthy Start grant. Because of its success, the center is working with four feeder elementary schools, one middle school, and one high school (to come on board at the end of 1995) in its cluster to disseminate the Vaughn approach.

When planning for the center began in 1991, Dr. Yvonne Chan, the school principal, saw it as a key to improving relations between the neighborhood's Latino and African American families. North Pacoima, where the school and the center are lo-

Continued on page 88

cated, has experienced rapid demographic shifts during the last decade as large numbers of Latinos have moved into what was a predominantly African American community. The tension between the two groups has been significant. Chan hoped the center would create areas of common ground as parents from both sides worked together to meet their children's basic needs.

Currently, seven of the 40 commission members are African American, and efforts to increase African American participation continue. One strategy has been to hold separate meetings of African American parents so that they would have opportunities to define the specific concerns facing their community. As the parents discussed the difficulties they faced, powerful feelings were unleashed. Family Center Director Yoland Trevino observes:

> "What I see happening is the development of self-awareness, discovering their own voice, the coming into their own sense of power and what happens with that first awakening. In my experience, that first awakening engenders a lot of anger. The veil is being lifted; they're realizing that they've been given the short end of the stick all these years. The next step is, what do you do with that? How do you help the parents come to the point that they continue to retain that passion and integrity about their own feelings, but at the same time transform these feelings into something constructive?"

One positive result of the meetings among the African American parents has been an emerging consensus that they want to focus on three major issues. First, they want their children to graduate from Vaughn with bilingual Spanish and English skills to help the youngsters communicate well and to expand future employment opportunities. Second, the parents want the school to present programs that em-

brace the cultural richness of the African American community. Third, they want their children to leave Vaughn as competent readers.

Building the level of parent participation and sense of community seen at Vaughn takes time and energy. "Parents need to feel valued before they're going to commit their valuable time," said Connie Dubin, one of the main architects who has stayed on full-time to continue developing the center. "Part of the process [of involving parents in the center's governance] is increasing the comfort and confidence level of the parents as they sit together with the providers." While the majority of providers are middle-class whites, most of the parents are low-income Latinos and African Americans. Parents who had previously interacted with whites only in work situations — with the white person clearly in charge — suddenly found themselves on equal footing.

The initial planners also recognized that many parents had never participated in formal meetings and needed background preparation. Well before the first commission meeting was held, parents were brought together for mock sessions so that they could become familiar with meeting procedures and rehearse their new roles. Before actual meetings, parents also get together as part of the Strategic Planning Team to decide which issues to present, another learning opportunity for them.

Trevino, the center's director, also makes it a point to take parents with her when she attends outside meetings. Gradually, parents have learned to go out on their own to make presentations in Trevino's absence. The progress has been palpable; parents see themselves as change agents able to have an impact on the service system.

Overall, finding common ground between Latinos and African Americans has proved challenging, but worth the effort. Latino parents say they welcome African American parent involvement and want all parents to have equal voice in decision-making. Both groups continue to discuss ways to change negative attitudes and stereotypes about each other and among their own children. They are looking for increased opportunities for African American parents to work hand-in-hand with Latino parents. Latino and African American parents realize that they must work with great sensitivity toward these goals.

Both groups acknowledge that stereotypes are not going to change overnight. Change begins in the home, and ultimately, the attitudes of the entire community will have to change. But as a start, the center provides opportunities for parents to meet socially and to learn about each other's cultures by sharing meals, music and cultural events, such as an evening jazz concert and musical in the school auditorium.

According to Trevino, the commission structure also places parents and teachers at the same table to discuss the needs of children. Parents no longer see themselves as relinquishing children to teachers. Parent Jorge Lara explains, "Parents have found that they can have a lot of power and say about what goes on at Vaughn and that the administration listens and respects their concerns." Another parent, Theresa Pantoja, added that everyone had ideas about how to change things at Vaughn. Parents used to be too shy and afraid to speak up, she said, but now the school's attitude is, "You count too. You're part of us and the system."

In turn, parents are more sure of their abilities to help their children with schoolwork, and they have greater confidence and motivation in seeking educational opportunities and advancement for themselves. Parent LaTonya Greathouse said, "When I first came here, I rarely spoke. Now you can't hardly shut me up. I came to see how I could become a volunteer. Now I am going for my GED and I am trying to get my husband to be involved."

The Family Center promotes parental involvement by the fact that it is run for parents and by parents, Trevino said. The center is also staffed by two Latino and one African American family advo-cates, as well as community liaisons. The parent involvement and capacity promoted in the center has slowly begun to reinforce participation in other school endeavors, especially restructuring efforts and the related, site-based management committee.

The center has helped build trust between parents and teachers, too. In the past, many teachers had been wary of allowing parents to visit their classrooms because it usually meant that the parents wanted to make a complaint. But the center has helped some teachers to understand that parents can be important resources in helping to educate children. For example, teacher Stephanie Moore brought in parents to assist students with science fair projects. Many parents ended up becoming friends and mentors to children other than their own. Although gaining trust hasn't happened easily with all teachers, parent Jorge Lara has noticed a definite change. "Now [teachers] treat the parents with welcome arms," he said. "Before, they would say, 'What do you want?' Their attitude has changed completely. Now they say, 'Can I help you?'"

Recently, the Vaughn school has embarked upon the process of becoming a charter school, which allows them to take over their own administration and budgeting. This new status has several implications for how decisions will be made at the school. Under the conditions of the charter, parents are entitled to make up a percentage of the governing team. To introduce parents to the complexities of running a school, the school staff and the Family Center have designed a parent leadership development course called "How the School Works." This course covers topics, such as budgeting, curriculum design, student assessment, and home-school relations. With such actions, the Vaughn community is stepping up to the challenge of community decision-making. Ultimately, it hopes that parents, teachers and service providers will take joint responsibility for their children.

6. The Continuing Challenges of Community Decision-Making

Vaughn is a wonderful illustration of the benefits which can be reaped through community governance. It ensures services are meaningful and relevant to the lives of the families being served. It increases buy-in and support. It builds a greater sense of community by allowing diverse groups opportunities to work together toward common objectives and gain a greater appreciation for each other's perspectives.

In the current political climate, developing effective strategies for involving community in decision-making is becoming increasingly important. Policymakers at all levels are showing interest in shifting funding decisions to the local level. For example, in 1993, the California legislature passed Assembly Bill 1741. This legislation allows five pilot counties to blend funding from a number of state categorical programs if they can provide the state with a strategic plan for children and family services. The plan must describe the goals and outcomes to which the counties are willing to be held accountable.

While shifting authority to the local level does not by itself assure that decisions will be made in partnership with communities, it can make it easier. Local decision-making often feels more accessible to community residents. People have an easier time getting to meetings, are more likely to know local officials and tend to see the decisions as immediately relevant to their neighborhoods. The danger of the current situation is that decision-making authority will shift but the community will still be left out because strategies are not undertaken to foster its participation. Clearly, much greater attention and resources need to be directed at efforts to develop, demonstrate and disseminate effective strategies for soliciting community involvement.

Our research also suggests that formal community involvement in governance is not by itself a sufficient strategy for ensuring the cultural and linguistic appropriateness of services. The previous sections of this reports are filled with descriptions of approaches which groups can use to take into account issues of race, language and culture and draw upon the knowledge of diverse perspectives. Some sites appeared able to improve the effectiveness of services without creating a community-governance structure. In some situations, managing the dynamics of a formal community-based governance body can even draw attention and resources away from other efforts to improve the quality of services. The question remains: To what extent, or when in the reform process, is community governance essential?

San Diego New Beginnings

A collaborative program experiences success in providing services to an elementary school's families. But now, it realizes that a new challenge lies ahead: building community self-sufficiency.

Located in an impoverished, high crime-area of San Diego, Hamilton Elementary School serves approximately 1,300 children in kindergarten through fifth grade and houses a state preschool program. The multiethnic student body, which includes many immigrants, is 43% Latino, 24% Southeast Asian, 22% African American, 8% white and 2% "other". More than 21 different languages are spoken by students. Hamilton, which has one of the highest mobility rates in the city, is a demonstration site for a new approach to delivering health and human services to families.

On the school grounds, a portable building houses the New Beginnings Center, which offers neighborhood families a wide range of assistance, including physical and mental health services, counseling, transportation, and eligibility assessments for AFDC, Food Stamps, Medicaid and WIC. The center is staffed by family services advocates, nurse practitioners, community workers and therapists who help families find the aid they need, either on-site or from other agencies.

The New Beginnings Center owes its existence to one simple phone call. Frustrated with the failures of the fragmented system of services, Richard "Jake" Jacobsen, who was director of the San Diego County Department of Social Services, called Tom Payzant, then Superintendent of the San Diego City Schools. The two men discussed how they might join forces to become more effective in addressing the needs of children and families. This conversation led quickly to the development of a collaborative partnership among six public entities: the San Diego County

Departments of Health, Probation, and Social Services, the San Diego Unified School District, City Manager's Office, and the Community College District.

Faced with shrinking budgets and growing demands, these partners recognized that single-agency solutions were not working. Instead, the partners realized that they shared responsibility for making sure families' needs were met, especially since some departments were working with the same households. From the onset, the New Beginnings effort has focused on developing closer working relationships among agencies, not only to produce innovative service strategies, but also to promote institutional changes.

When the collaborative decided to focus on Hamilton, it began by identifying services currently available to families. Then it analyzed family needs, barriers to services, and ways to make the delivery system more cost-effective and integrated. The collaborative used several methods to gather information, including family interviews, focus groups with line workers and parents to discover the most pressing needs, and data gathered by a Spanish-speaking social worker outstationed at Hamilton for three months. The collaborative also matched school data with files maintained by the Department of Social Services, Probation and Housing Commission. This data match, financed with additional support from the Stuart Foundations, proved critical and compel-

Continued on page 92

ling. By documenting that the Department of Social Services had spent $5.7 million in services at Hamilton in one year, the collaborative provided strong justification for re-allocating agency staff to work at the school.

Eventually, the six original partners expanded their vision and began to identify other stakeholders who could provide important missing resources. As a result, new members came aboard: the University of California at San Diego Medical Center, Children's Hospital, the Housing Commission, Head Start, and a community-based agency called Home Start.

Currently, the New Beginnings effort is overseen by a multi-level governance structure. The agency heads, who form the Executive Committee, make final budget and policy decisions, but the collaborative's nuts-and-bolts work is carried out by a council consisting of high-level managers from each agency. Council responsibilities have included establishing community assessment and staff orientation procedures; investigating confidentiality issues; developing an appropriate system of program evaluation; and reviewing relevant legislation. At the site level, center Director Connie Busse is in charge of program administration, with support from school principal Carrie Perry and Dr. Sandra Daley, a physician who oversees health services part-time .

Multiethnic Workers Reach Out to Families

Given the multilingual, multiethnic nature of Hamilton's families, the challenge of developing a center capable of meeting the needs of such a diverse population was discussed heavily among those responsible for implementation. According to Department of Social Services Deputy Director Connie Roberts, considerations included the hiring of multiethnic workers and even details such as the center's decor. Attention to Hamilton's diversity, she said, "is embedded in the essence of center operations and staffing."

New Beginnings found that employing staff from the communities being served has been critical to effective services. The Hamilton model's most recent move has been to hire community outreach workers. These new employees, who complement the center's regular family support advocates, come from Vietnamese, Hmong, African American and Mexican American backgrounds.

To date, the center has found that Asian families use services less than other groups. But their usage has increased significantly with the hiring of the Hmong and Vietnamese community outreach workers, whose familiarity with language and culture serve as effective entry points. Vietnamese outreach worker Marlene Nguyen explains, "My policy is to establish trust with the parents first. If the parent talks simple, then I talk simple. It is important to act sincere and respect parents as they are. If they talk simply and I talk sophisticated, they won't like me."

One concrete result of this outreach strategy is that the center has become a resource for a small number of Southeast Asian women who are victims of domestic violence. Winning the women's trust was no small feat, considering their strong cultural taboo against going outside the family for support. Center Director Connie Busse recognizes the importance of reflective staffing. She believes that adding a Cambodian worker is critical to increasing outreach to the Cambodian community, and she remains concerned that the center still lacks an African American family support advocate.

The Need to Foster Self-Sufficiency

Recently, however, New Beginnings' philosophy on serving the Hamilton community has begun to evolve. Many of the leaders who helped create the center have realized that a model based primarily on agency collaboration and services is limited in impact because it overlooks the need to build the community's capacity for self-sufficiency and advocacy on its own behalf. Reflecting back, Social Services Deputy Director Connie Roberts says:

"When we began, we focused on the physical center and getting the direct services going. It wasn't like the community was ignored. The problem was the community piece was always assumed to be a part of the planning but never was a particular focus of the Phase I, Phase II, Phase III plans....We now realize that no matter how well we integrate services, how many agencies are involved, it's not enough."

Council member Leslie Hine-Rabichow adds:

"The movement is steering away from deficit-based to strength-based community. It is becoming more than providing individual services. The language and focus is changing, and community development is directly related."

For Dr. Sandra Daley, who oversees New Beginnings' health services, the hope for change lies in building the community's capacity to advocate for itself.

"I spent 12 years as a physician in a community health center. I realized that health services at the center were less likely to undergo funding cuts if I had a large group of regular people who use the services scream, 'Don't cut! Don't cut!' The problem is that many of the people in underserved communities simply don't know how to scream. The community workers are my way of addressing this problem. Under the guise of providing health information, which we will train them to do, they will also start to provide a structure for creating neighborhood groups, that are aware of what is going on in their community and of some of the resources available to them to address the issues they identify."

As a first step toward building families' self-sufficiency, New Beginnings has begun empowering parents to support the growth and development of their children. The center has dispatched its multiethnic community workers to teach parents the principles of the national "Parents As Teachers" (PAT) program. When teaching the PAT program to parents, the community workers also will solicit feedback to discern whether its curriculum is culturally relevant.

Continued Success Requires Institutional Reform

Just as the New Beginnings center has provided insight into the complexities of developing a system that truly responds to the needs of a multiethnic community, the effort as a whole has offered lessons about the challenges of maintaining support for institutional reform. In the past few years, New Beginnings has seen dramatic changeover among the key agency executives who initiated the effort and committed the original resources. As new faces assume key positions, New Beginnings must find ways to familiarize incoming executives with the work of the initiative, gain their commitment, and ensure that a sense of trust and teamwork continues to develop among all the agencies.

The loss of the original executives who inspired New Beginnings is also forcing council members to reconsider an earlier decision to avoid direct involvement of elected officials. The original partners felt it was important to keep elected officials informed, but unwise to encourage any active involvement. They feared the project might become the pet project of a particular official and thus arouse rivals and opposition. This approach has some downsides, however. Janlee Wong of the County Administrator's office explains:

"You can get things done very quickly, outside of elected officials and the political process...The weakness is there is not enough institutionalization. If you don't go through the policy board [e.g. Board of Supervisors or School Board], how do you keep it in the budget and commit staff? Without policy board buy-in, it is only through the discretion of the (agency) department head. This raises the question of how to institutionalize the effort and make it long-lasting, particularly after the department heads change."

The New Beginnings Council now feels it needs to pay more attention to ensuring that the policy boards are engaged enough in the initiative to give it the support needed for institutionalization.

CHAPTER 7

Conclusion and Recommendations

A s the United States continues to grow more racially, culturally and linguistically diverse, many voices are calling upon this nation to rise to the challenges of building a fair, working, multiethnic society. But achieving this goal requires that we lay new foundations in every corner of public life.

In the human services field, many of the old foundations — which were constructed for a less diverse society — have grown weak and ineffective. Providing effective services and supports for our newly emerging society will require drawing strength from the cultural, linguistic, and racial diversity of families and communities. Underlying this report are a set of core principles:

♦ Supporting the healthy development of families and communities requires valuing and respecting their languages and cultures.

♦ Diversity and unity are inter-related themes. Opportunities must be provided for individuals to: (1) build a strong sense of ethnic identity and group consciousness with members of their own group, and (2) find common ground across diverse backgrounds.

♦ Disaggregated data (broken down by race, language, gender and other relevant criteria) is critical for discovering which approaches and programs work for which types of families. Such data can also uncover practices that may have detrimental impact on certain groups.

♦ Developing effective supports entails drawing upon the insight, knowledge and skills of community members whose experiences might include overcoming racism or growing up within a particular cultural or linguistic group.

♦ To ensure that diverse community voices contribute to the reform process, service providers must: (1) foster the community's capacity to advocate for itself and to participate in decision-making over the long term, and (2) build the capacity of institutions to work in partnership with community members.

♦ Drawing upon the strengths of diversity requires much more than examining issues of individual bias or discrimination. It entails a larger-scale assessment of the policies and practices of agencies and systems.

♦ The human services system cannot be held accountable for outcomes unless there are people capable of holding it accountable. Institutional change of this nature requires that parents, youths, community representatives, service providers, agency heads, policymakers, facilitators and other change agents develop new leadership skills, including the ability to monitor the system's effectiveness.

Reform initiatives offer tremendous opportunities to address issues of diversity.

These themes, which are raised in the various chapters, underscore a major premise of this report: efforts to reform services for children and families are inextricably linked to issues of diversity.

Reform initiatives offer tremendous opportunities to address issues of diversity because they open the door for communities and families to be involved in designing and developing a comprehensive array of services and supports. The reform process also encourages policy-makers and providers to reflect upon whether the types of services they wish to provide are appropriate, given the ethnic diversity of families served.

At the same time, the reform movement will not lead to improved outcomes for families and communities unless attention to diversity becomes a central theme. Issues of diversity are essential at every point, from the community assessment process to the equipping of agency staff and the formation of an inclusive governance structure. Issues of diversity cannot be treated as afterthoughts that have only minor relevance to the central elements of a reform agenda.

This report is offered as a catalyst for dialogue and a call to action. Despite the volatility and deep pain that can arise when discussing issues of diversity and equity, our society can no longer afford to avoid these subjects. We need to develop the forums that will allow us to draw upon the lessons learned from our diverse communities and forge ahead with new strategies for improving conditions for children and families. We can no longer pay the price of failing to create the supports and services that will promote the healthy development of all families.

We all must take responsibility for working to improve outcomes for children and families.

Recommendations for Immediate Action

Everyone has a role in reforming the human services system to be truly responsive to diverse communities. We all must take responsibility for working to improve outcomes for children and families. While the recommendations below are addressed to different groups, it is important to recognize that many of the goals cannot be achieved by one group acting alone. For example, holding institutions accountable for serving diverse communities effectively is a collective effort involving funders, different levels of government, community-based organizations, advocates, community members, and evaluators — each group is crucial. Similarly, no one group can design and develop culturally and linguistically appropriate services without assistance from other groups, whether help comes in the form of expertise, experience or resources. Because of these interconnections, we have deliberately made the same recommendations to several groups with the knowledge that moving ahead will require coordination across the various sectors. In order to move the human services reform movement to address issues of diversity, we recommend:

1. Federal Government

a. Fund the development of data collection systems that disaggregate data by race, ethnicity, language and gender in order to monitor the effectiveness of services and programs for all ethnic and language groups.

b. Develop criteria to assess whether services are culturally and linguistically appropriate.

c. Require that state plans for integrating services demonstrate how they will adapt services to respond to the cultures and languages of families and how they will ensure access to services for cultural and linguistic minorities.

d. Require states to show how supports and services are achieving their goals and objectives and improving outcomes for children and families in diverse communities.

2. California State Government and Legislature

a. State-level collaboratives and public agencies must seek the input and backing of diverse community representatives in designing services and supports for children and families.

b. Develop criteria to assess whether services are culturally and linguistically appropriate.

c. For initiatives that shift resources and responsibilities for overseeing health and human services programs from the state level to the local level, the state should require the following:

(1) county plans that describe how providers will ensure that services are responsive to the cultures and languages of diverse families served; plans also must describe how access to services will be assured for all diverse groups.

(2) if the state requires the development of outcomes, counties must include community representatives in defining outcomes appropriate to the community; furthermore, outcomes measures should allow for monitoring the effectiveness of services and programs for all language and culture groups.

d. Coordinate existing technical assistance efforts to develop and disseminate effective strategies for working with diverse communities.

e. Establish an interdisciplinary and multicultural task force to:

(1) assess professional development opportunities for human services staff who work with diverse families. The assessment should analyze the available resources for professional development among departments.

(2) develop a plan, based on the assessment of resources, for ensuring that staff receive adequate pre-service and in-service professional development opportunities. Elements of the professional development plan should address how to:

- incorporate principles of family support (e.g. building on the strengths of families)

- create partnerships with parents

- adapt services to respond to the cultures and languages of families

- improve access to services for cultural and linguistic minorities

- work in interdisciplinary teams

- gather and use client feedback/data to inform practice and improve services

f. Establish an interagency task force to investigate the extent to which credentialing policies and practices pose barriers to hiring staff with knowledge and expertise about diverse children and families. The task force should develop specific recommendations to address any identified barriers.

3. County and Municipal Government

a. Develop data collection systems that disaggregate data by race, ethnicity, language, and gender to monitor effectiveness of services and programs for all ethnic and language groups. These data should be made available and accessible, in clear and understandable forms, to agency staff, community-based organizations, advocates and community residents.

b. Use assessments of client satisfaction to detect problems with staff responsiveness to particular populations.

c. Assess extent to which staffs reflect the language and cultural backgrounds of the families they serve. If staff is not reflective, agencies must eliminate any identified institutional barriers and develop a plan for the successful recruitment and retention of appropriate staff.

d. Develop an agency plan for assessing and improving professional development activities that strengthen the ability of line staff and administrators to:

(1) work in multiracial, interdisciplinary teams; and

(2) engage in strategies for working effectively with culturally and linguistically diverse children and families. This plan should not view diversity training as a separate component or one-time event, but should be woven throughout the agency's professional development plan. Individual agencies should coordinate their plan with those of other public and private services organizations and agencies in order to make maximum use of limited resources.

e. Assess whether personnel procedures and requirements:

(1) reward staff and administrators who demonstrate the ability to work in diverse settings, or

(2) create unnecessary barriers to recruiting or hiring culturally and linguistically appropriate staff.

f. Before making a major staffing decision, such as cutting staff based on seniority or offering an early retirement plan, decision-makers must analyze whether the change would enhance or reduce an organization's ability to serve different ethnic and linguistic populations effectively.

g. Develop strategies for getting community input on design and development of services. Include service recipients on every respective collaborative task force, committee, and commission.

4. County/Local Collaboratives

a. Collect and disseminate information already available on the resources, needs and conditions of various ethnic and linguistic populations. Such information should be available to public agencies, non-profits, community groups and any other individuals and organizations.

b. Analyze existing data and work with other collaborative members to determine what additional information is needed about various ethnic and linguistic populations in order to design more effective programs. Develop strategies to fill any information gaps.

c. Coordinate the professional development plans of separate organizations to strengthen the ability of line staff and administrators to:

(1) work in multiracial, interdisciplinary teams; and

(2) engage in strategies for effectively working with culturally and linguistically diverse children and families. This approach should not view diversity training as a separate component or one-time event, but should be woven throughout the agency's professional development plan. Individual agencies should coordinate their plan with those of other public and private services organizations and agencies in order to make maximum use of limited resources.

d. Create opportunities for the most disenfranchised groups to participate in decision-making. This task may include investing in leadership development activities that build community members' capacity to participate.

e. Collect and disseminate information about strategies that public and private agencies have used to improve effectiveness in working with diverse populations (e.g. changing job classifications to reward staff for their expertise and special skills in language and culture). Collaboratives should actively promote these strategies across agencies.

5. Community-Based Service Providers

a. Develop data collection systems that disaggregate data by race, ethnicity, language, and gender in order to monitor the effectiveness of services and programs for all ethnic and language groups. All such data should be made available and accessible, in clear and understandable forms, to agency staff, advocates and community residents.

b. Use various types of assessments of client satisfaction — focus groups, individual interviews, written surveys in clients' languages — to detect problems with staff responsiveness to particular populations.

c. Assess the extent to which staff members reflect the language and cultural backgrounds of the families they serve. If staff is not reflective, agencies must eliminate any identified institutional barriers and develop a plan for the successful recruitment and retention of appropriate staff.

d. Develop an organization plan for assessing and improving professional development activities that strengthen the ability of line staff and administrators to:

(1) work in multiracial, interdisciplinary teams; and

(2) engage in strategies for working effectively with culturally and linguistically diverse children and families. This plan should not view diversity training as a separate component or one-time event, but should be woven throughout the agency's professional development plan. Coordinate the plan with other public and private services organizations and agencies in order to make maximum use of limited resources.

e. Assess whether personnel guidelines reward staff and administrators who demonstrate ability to work in diverse settings.

f. Before making a major staffing decision, such as cutting staff based on seniority or offering an early retirement plan, analyze whether the decision would enhance or reduce the ability of the organization to serve different ethnic and linguistic populations effectively.

g. Develop strategies for getting community input on the design and development of services. Include service recipients on every respective collaborative task force, committee, and commission.

h. Provide training and education to clients to enhance their leadership capacity to be community advocates.

6. Community-Based Advocates

a. Work in partnership with community residents, parents, youth and others to analyze data on the effectiveness of services. This information should be used to hold agencies accountable for providing culturally and linguistically appropriate services to diverse groups of children and families.

b. Provide community residents, parents, youth and others with education and training for developing leadership and advocacy skills.

7. Community Members

a. Work in partnership with agencies to identify and use informal resources and supports within communities.

b. Build coalitions and find common ground with other community members (including parents) across lines of race and ethnicity. This will strengthen advocacy for effective services and supports.

c. Take an active role in requesting and monitoring data from agencies regarding how well their services have improved conditions for children and families as a whole, and for relevant sub-categories as defined by race, gender, language background, etc.

8. Funders (Government and Private Foundations)

a. Increase internal capacity to understand issues of diversity through staff development activities.

b. Recruit, hire and retain ethnically diverse staff who have extensive experience working in diverse communities.

c. Fund programs that are developing or providing culturally and linguistically appropriate services. (Conversely, funders should not support programs that provide culturally or linguistically inappropriate services.) To promote appropriate programs, funders may need to revise funding criteria to give priority to grantees that:

(1) look at data disaggregated by race and language, then describe how they will take this information into account when designing and implementing services and programs.

(2) describe how their work will foster and draw upon the resources and strengths that they have identified in the diverse populations targeted.

(3) discuss how they will ensure the representation of diverse groups in decision-making.

(4) explain how their proposed activities reflect outcomes, strategies and concerns identified by the community members who will be served.

d. Fund technical assistance and training designed to help individuals and organizations engaged in reform efforts to analyze the implications of disaggregated data, identify strengths of different ethnic groups, and develop collaborative processes that engage diverse community representatives.

e. Fund technical assistance, staff development and networking efforts designed to build the capacity of organizations at all levels, such as public agencies and community-based organizations, to work in partnership with families and communities to design appropriate services and programs.

f. Fund capacity and leadership development programs for community residents to become effective advocates and responsible decision-makers.

g. Fund the development and implementation of evaluation strategies that encourage agencies to engage in self-reflective practice, particularly for developing their ability to work with ethnically and linguistically diverse populations.

h. Fund the development and implementation of a cross-agency evaluation system that uses outcomes to assess which types of programs, agencies and strategies are most effective in working with ethnically and linguistically diverse populations — both for an individual ethnic group, and on a collective basis. Over time, such data can be used as the basis for future funding decisions.

9. Institutions of Higher Learning

a. Reform pre-service curriculum to produce a generation of human service providers and educators who have the skills to draw upon the strengths of children and families from different cultures, work across agencies, and work in partnership with communities.

b. Develop student practicum designed to expose students to innovative collaborative efforts, and create opportunities for collaborative efforts to draw upon the perspectives of students who come from the communities being served.

c. Enter into partnerships with communities, such as developing evaluation projects aimed at helping communities to engage in reflective practice.

d. Reform curriculum for teaching evaluation skills to students. The new curriculum must foster the development of "process" skills, which enable evaluators to work with diverse communities in designing culturally appropriate assessment tools.

e. Develop strategies for recruiting and retaining students from under-represented groups in order to better serve ethnic and linguistic communities.

10. Schools and School Districts

Forge new partnerships with community-based organizations and public agencies to provide responsive, culturally and linguistically appropriate, school-linked services for children, youth and families. In doing so, schools and school districts should:

a. Conduct an assessment of the strengths and needs of children and families, as well as community and school resources. The assessment of school resources should encompass existing pupil support services, such as student study teams, school social workers, the Senate Bill 65 (dropout) coordinator and others.

b. Analyze the availability and appropriateness of services for various ethnic and linguistic groups in the school community.

c. Create forums for school administrators, teachers, school support staff, parents and service providers to:

(1) discuss how supports and resources need to be created or reconfigured, and

(2) develop criteria for identifying students and families who would benefit most from services.

d. Involve community-based organizations that serve the students' communities and can offer critical insights about how to provide culturally and linguistically appropriate services.

11. Diversity Trainers

a. Work with agencies to develop and incorporate an on-going diversity training component into the overall organizational staff development plan.

b. Work with agencies to define the specific issues to be addressed through workshops and training.

Recommendations for Future Research

1. Community governance offers one broad area for additional research. Some questions to explore: What strategies will work in "communities" that lack cohesiveness among ethnic groups? How critical a strategy is community governance within the larger effort to improve the cultural and linguistic appropriateness of services?

2. A second area that deserves further research and model development: Can collaborative services initiatives have impact on community economic development, community organizing, and the empowerment and self-sufficiency of families? Are they doing so already? If so, to what extent do such initiatives overlap and combine to address diverse community needs?

APPENDIX A

Research Methodology

This publication draws primarily upon research conducted between January and October 1993. Research components included: a) a survey of 98 collaborative programs in California, b) site visits to seven collaborative programs — six in California, one in Colorado — that took thoughtful approaches to incorporating issues of diversity into their reform efforts, c) in-depth interviews with individuals around the country who are involved in collaborative reform initiatives, and d) a literature review. This report also draws upon California Tomorrow's five years of experience in working on issues related to interagency collaboration and integrated health and human services. Funded by the Stuart Foundations, our work has involved: operating a clearinghouse of resource materials, providing technical assistance to selected communities, convening a network of technical assistance providers, developing selected resource materials, and using information gleaned from these activities to influence state and local policy.

The Survey

As part of our earlier clearinghouse work, we identified 230 programs in California that used interagency collaboration to provide a comprehensive array of services to children and families. These included a variety of program types. Some linked services to schools or integrated services for particular target populations, while others were interagency efforts generally seeking to coordinate policies and programs across the array of agencies serving children and families. Surveys were sent to all these programs in Spring 1993.

Approximately 43% of surveys were returned, a total of 98 responses. Of this group, 55% (or 54 programs) operated in urban areas, and 11% (or 11 programs) were located in rural areas. Programs in suburbs accounted for another 11% (or 11 programs). Last of all, 22% indicated that the geographic area they served was a mix of urban, rural and suburban.

The collaboratives surveyed relied upon a patchwork of funding sources to keep themselves operational. Private foundations had contributed support to 32% of programs surveyed, corporations, 14%.

A large majority of the collaboratives, or 85%, were publicly funded: 40% had received federal funding; 63% had received state funding, with the majority (half of all programs surveyed) being funded by California's Healthy Start initiative. Collaboratives also enjoyed significant support from local government: 32% from counties, 33% from school districts, and 16% from cities.

To increase cooperation among groups that run similar clearinghouses, California Tomorrow designed the survey in collaboration with the National Center for Service Integration in Washington D.C. and the Family Resource Coalition in Chicago. The survey asked collaboratives for a wide array of information about program services, types of organizations involved, staffing, funding sources and populations served. (See Appendix B for a copy of the survey) We used the demographic information to assess the extent to which collaboratives were staffed and governed by individuals who reflected the racial and linguistic background of the children, youth and families served. The survey also yielded information about the types of organizations and groups involved in governance, and whether collaboratives had conducted community assessments.

Site Visits

California Tomorrow visited seven sites. Six of the programs were in California. These included: Casa Loma (Los Angeles County, CA), Family Mosaic (San Francisco County, CA), New Beginnings (San Diego County, CA), Sacramento County Human Services Reorganization, (Sacramento County, CA), Vaughn Family Center (Los Angeles County, CA), and Yuba County Coordinated Services Project, (Yuba County, CA). We also selected one site, the Family Resource Schools in Denver, Colorado, to give us some sense of whether the issues arising in California were also playing out in other parts of the country. California Tomorrow staff or colleagues working on human service reforms had identified these sites as conscious efforts to address issues of diversity. Collectively, the sites represented a broad distribution in terms of geography, location of service delivery (school, public housing complex, public agency offices), lead agency (non-profit, school, public agency), and scale of operations (e.g. county-wide vs. single site).

Site visits were conducted by multiethnic teams of three to four California Tomorrow researchers. Most visits took two days. The purpose of the site visits was to provide the team with an overall picture of program operations and information about a number of specific issues. For example, to what extent did the individuals involved in the initiative openly discuss issues of racial, linguistic, or cultural diversity? If no dialogue was occurring, what barriers were preventing such discussion? If these discussions were occurring, what factors made it possible for the group to talk about race, language and culture? What kinds of diversity issues arose? What strategies did the group use to address them? To what extent were community members or parents involved in shaping the initiative or the types of services and supports provided? How did issues of diversity affect the ability of the collaborative to involve community members? What did interviewees think were the greatest challenges to moving forward with their work?

At each site, researchers sought interviews with family members (children, youth and parents) from the different ethnic populations being served, as well as a cross-section of staff, program coordinators, mid-level managers, agency heads, and local policymakers. Altogether, California Tomorrow researchers interviewed 190 people individually or in small groups. Interviewing the diverse constituencies involved in the implementation of an initiative was a crucial site visit strategy that allowed us to compare how different types of individuals perceived what was happening at the site. The team also collected pertinent written materials, such as evaluations, reports, proposals or program brochures.

At four of the sites, California Tomorrow also arranged subsequent meetings to discuss the findings of our visit with the coordinators or the collaborative's policymaking group. These debriefing sessions were a concrete demonstration of our belief that site visits are a mutual learning process. As researchers, site visits deepen our thinking and understanding of the challenges, strategies and realities of local communities. At the same time, we wanted sites to be able to benefit from our insights. Because of our neutral position as "outsiders" and our comprehensive approach to collecting information, we felt that we could sometimes detect issues that might be overlooked by individuals immersed in the details of implementation. These debriefing sessions provided California Tomorrow staff with an opportunity to check whether our observation matched the perceptions of the individuals involved in implementation. The sessions also allowed us to offer our feedback on strengths and concerns. California Tomorrow staff felt this approach ensured that the research could be used to further the growth and development of the participating sites.

Individual Interviews

To gain a broader sense of the field, California Tomorrow interviewed an additional 38 individuals involved in human service reform initiatives in California or other parts of the nation. These persons had been identified by California Tomorrow staff or nominated by colleagues for their thoughtful approaches to issues of diversity in their work. Of those interviewed, 18 coordinated or directed a site-level effort, 4 were mid-level agency administrators, 3 were evaluators, and 13 provided technical assistance. Interviews were designed to solicit information about these individuals' professional backgrounds, their sense of how issues of diversity were arising in their work, and the strategies they used to address them. Most interviews were conducted over the telephone. A few were held in person. Typically, interviews took between 30 and 90 minutes.

Literature Review

Most of the literature review involved examining whether issues of diversity were discussed in current publications on interagency collaboration, integrating services for children, or reforming health and human services. Because information gleaned through this process was scarce, California Tomorrow staff also used the search as an opportunity to collect information about cultural, racial and linguistic diversity from particular disciplines, such as mental health, social work or early childhood education.

The Analysis

In mid-October, we convened 22 individuals for a two-day retreat to review the preliminary findings of these three components: the survey, site visits and individual interviews. Participants discussed the findings and delved into issues requiring further exploration, such as: community governance, the implications of diversity for program evaluation, the role of community-based organizations, the infusion of diversity into training activities, and allocation of resources to ensure effective services for diverse populations.

Retreat participants encompassed a broad array of ethnic and disciplinary backgrounds. They included technical assistance providers, evaluators, foundation officers, project coordinators, and agency administrators. (See Acknowledgments for list of participants) Through our site visits, individual interviews and general work on collaborative services, we were able to select these participants for their familiarity with diversity issues and understanding of current human service reform efforts.

The initial draft of this report was also reviewed extensively by more than 50 readers, including retreat participants, California Tomorrow's Board of Directors, and others actively involved in the reform movement. Comments on the draft were provided in writing and through follow-up phone calls with California Tomorrow staff. The report was significantly revised as a result of this input.

Collaborative Services Organizations Survey

I. General Information

Program Name:

Address:

City/State/Zip code:

Telephone Number: FAX:

Electronic bulletin board: E-mail address:

Key Contact Person: Title:

Name of Person Completing Survey:

Title: Telephone Number:

What year was the program established?

II. Collaborative Program Information

A. Please read all the purposes for the programs listed below. Select the MAIN reason why your program exists and write a "1" on the line in front of the program's primary purpose. Write a "2" on the line in front of all non-primary purposes of the program that apply. Select as many secondary purposes as are applicable.

__ Coordinate available, existing services
__ Provide comprehensive health, educational and social services
__ Provide health care
__ Improve access to health care
__ Improve children's mental health
__ Prevent child abuse or neglect
__ Enhance parental knowledge, attitudes and skills in the development of children
__ Promote family growth toward economic self-sufficiency
__ Provide support for teenage parents
__ Address issues of family violence
__ Prevent the placement of children in foster care (family preservation, family reunification)
__ Address alcohol or other drug abuse
__ Create safe neighborhoods and schools (prevent gang activities)
__ Increase academic performance of children
__ Address school failure/dropout (school readiness, preparation for school success or re-entry into schools for dropouts)

__ Increase parental involvement in child's education or school

__ Increase client knowledge of and access to existing services (teaching the client to be his/her own advocate)

__ Change existing policies for children and families at the local level

__ Change existing policies for children and families at the state level

__ Change existing policies for children and families at the federal level

__ Conduct research on topics related to children and families

__ Provide training and technical assistance

__ Other _____

B. Interagency efforts exist at a variety of levels. While some are focused on actually providing a comprehensive array of services, others are primarily directed at changing policies which inhibit service coordination. Others combine both direct services and policy work. In order to help us understand the purposes for your interagency effort, please check the statement which BEST describes your interagency effort: (CHECK ONE ONLY)

__ We are primarily dedicated to coordinating and changing policies across children and family serving agencies. We do not provide direct services.

__ We work primarily at the service delivery level to provide an integrated array of services to children and families. We are not linked to an interagency body which includes high-level agency representatives with decision-making authority.

__ We work primarily at the service delivery level to provide an integrated array of services to children and families AND are linked to an interagency body which includes high-level agency representatives with decision-making authority. This interagency body is called (Please fill in).

__ We dedicate an equal amount of effort to coordinating and changing policies across children and family serving agencies AND directly providing an integrated array of services to children and families.

C.1. What types of agencies are involved in your program?

a. Public agencies that perform the following functions: (CHECK ALL WHICH APPLY AND WRITE IN THE NAME OF THE AGENCY TO THE RIGHT)

NAME OF AGENCY (NO ACRONYMS, PLEASE)

__ Child Welfare/Protective Services _____

__ Education _____

__ Employment/Labor _____

__ Health _____

__ Juvenile Justice _____

__ Mental Health _____

__ Parks and Recreation _____

__ Public Housing _____

__ Public Libraries _____

__ Welfare/Income Maintenance _____

__ Other (Please describe) _____

b. Community-based/Non-profit agencies: (please list, attach an additional sheet if necessary)

_____

_____

_____

c. Businesses? __ Yes __ No

2. Is there a lead, administrative or host agency?

__ No __Yes. If so, please list the agency name and address:

Agency name: _____

Address: _____

City/State/Zip: _____

3. At what level did the impetus for your collaborative occur?
   __ State
   __ County
   __ Local
   __ Not sure

4. Is the working relationship between agencies in your collaborative informal or formal?
   __ Informal agreement
   __ Formal, written agreement (CHECK ALL THAT APPLY)
      __ Contract
      __ Memorandum of understanding or Interagency agreement
      __ Other (DESCRIBE)_____
   __ Not sure

5. In what type of community is your interagency program located?
   __ Mega Urban (population of one million or greater)
   __ Urban
   __ Suburban
   __ Rural
   __ Mixed (Please describe)

6. Are services offered at multiple sites, or just one site?
   __ Multiple sites
   __ Single site

7. What is (are) the site(s) of service delivery? (CHECK ALL THAT APPLY)
__ School
__ Home
__ Agency (Public)
__ Community-based non-profit agency
__ Church/synagogue
__ Day care, pre-school, Head Start program
__ Hospital/health clinic
__ Library
__ Mental health center
__ Military base
__ Museum
__ Prison
__ University/community college
__ Workplace
__ Other (DESCRIBE)_____

8. What services does your program provide on a regular basis?
(PLEASE CHECK ALL THE SERVICES THAT APPLY TO YOUR PROGRAM AND INDICATE WHETHER EACH SERVICE IS PROVIDED DIRECTLY BY YOUR PROGRAM, INDIRECTLY THROUGH REFERRALS OR WILL BE PROVIDED ONCE YOUR PROGRAM IS OPERATIONAL)

Services	Provided Directly	Referrals	Plan to Provide
__ Adult education			
__ Case management			
__ Individual case manager			
__ Case management by a team of providers			
__ Other			
__ Childcare			
__ Child development activities			
__ Counseling			
__ Academic			
__ Crisis			
__ Psychiatric			
__ Individual			
__ Family			
__ Crisis Intervention			
__ Hotline for assistance in crises			

Services	Provided Directly	Referrals	Plan to Provide
__ Developmental screening for children			
__ Drop-in			
__ Eligibility assessments for			
__ AFDC			
__ Food Stamps			
__ Medicaid			
__ WIC			
__ GED/High school diploma			
__ Health Care			
__ Dental services			
__ Health screenings			
__ Prenatal care			
__ Primary care			
__ Immunizations			
__ Contraceptives			
__ HIV testing			
__ Other _____			
__ Mental Health services			
__ Housing assistance			
__ Job training			
__ Legal assistance			
__ Newsletters and other educational & informational materials			
__ Nutrition services			
__ Parent-child activities			
__ Parenting skills			
__ Parent support groups			
__ Peer counseling			
__ Personal/life skills (e.g. stress management or budgeting)			
__ Respite childcare			
__ Social/recreational activities			

Services	Provided Directly	Referrals	Plan to Provide
__ Student support groups			
__ Substance abuse education and treatment services			
__ Transportation			
__ Translation services			
__ Tutoring			
__ Vocational education			
__ Warmline for general support			
__ Other			

D.1. Is your program a pilot program? (That is, has it been funded for a limited period of time?)
   __ No __Yes If yes, how many years will the funding last? _____

2. Have you ever done an assessment of community needs and resources?
   __ Yes __ No

3. Have you ever done a needs assessment for particular populations?
   __ Yes __ No

4. Has your program been evaluated?
   __ Yes __ No
      If yes, answer #5 below. If no, skip question #5

5. How was your program evaluated?
   __ Outside, third-party evaluation
   __ Funding source evaluation
   __ Internal or self evaluation
   __ Client/family evaluation

6. Do you use a common intake/assessment form?
   __ Yes __ No

7. Is there a formal system for on-going client feedback?

    __ No __ Yes (Please check which ones)

                        __ Surveys

                        __ Focus groups

                        __ Follow-up phone calls

                        __ Suggestion boxes

                        __ Other

8. Are you working on changing eligibility rules in order to eliminate conflicting requirements?

    __ Yes __ No

9. Do you engage in cross-disciplinary staff development?

    __ Yes __ No

10. Do you know of any efforts to replicate your program?

    __ Yes __ No

III. Staffing for Your Collaborative Program

1. How many staff does your collaborative have (both full-time and part-time)?

    __FT __ PT

2. Does your collaborative have a director or coordinator?

    __ Yes __ No

3. What is his/her professional background? (CHECK ALL APPLICABLE CATEGORIES)

    __ Education

    __ Child Care/Development

    __ Clergy

    __ Social Services

    __ Health

    __ Mental Health

    __ Juvenile Justice

    __ Community Advocacy

    __ Other

4. Is the director Male or Female? _____

5. What is his/her race/ethnicity? _____

6. Excluding the director, how many of the collaborative staff are male? Female? M_____   F_____

7. How many of your staff come from the following racial/ethnic groups? (Please write in the number of staff members that fall into each category. The number of staff for each major category should equal the total of the subcategories. For example, if your staff includes one Cambodian, one Chinese and one Korean, you should write "1" beside each subcategory and a total of "3" under the major category of Asian/Pacific Islander.)

__ Asian/Pacific Islander   __ Caucasian/White
   __ Cambodian
   __ Chinese   __ Latino/Hispanic
   __ Hmong   __ Central American
   __ Indian   __ Cuban
   __ Japanese   __ Mexican
   __ Korean   __ Puerto Rican
   __ Pacific Islander   __ South American
   __ Vietnamese
   __ Other   __ Native American

__ Black   __ Mixed Ethnicity
   __ African
   __ African-American   __ Other
   __ Caribbean

8. What languages do people on your staff use in speaking with clients? (CHECK ALL THAT APPLY):
   __ Armenian
   __ Cambodian
   __ Chinese (Cantonese, Mandarin, other dialect)
   __ English
   __ Filipino/Tagalog
   __ French
   __ Hmong
   __ Korean
   __ Russian
   __ Spanish
   __ Vietnamese
   __ Other

IV. Governance for the Collaborative Program

We would like you to describe by answering the questions below the body primarily responsible for making policy and programming decisions, whether you call it a board, steering committee or something else.

A. Name of your governing body _____

B. How many people are in this group?_____

C. What groups do they represent? (CHECK ALL THAT APPLY)
___ clients/consumers
___ public agencies
___ community-based/non-profit agencies
___ parents (no agency affiliation)
___ students
___ other (please describe)

D. How many are male?_____ Female?_____

E. How many of the members of come from the following racial/ethnic groups? (Please write in the number of members that fall into each category. The number of members for each major category should equal the total of the subcategories. For example, if your governing body includes one Cambodian, one Chinese and one Korean, you should write "1" beside each subcategory and a total of "3" under the major category of Asian/Pacific Islander.)

___ Asian/Pacific Islander
    ___ Cambodian
    ___ Chinese
    ___ Hmong
    ___ Indian
    ___ Japanese
    ___ Korean
    ___ Pacific Islander
    ___ Vietnamese
    ___ Other

___ Black
    ___ African
    ___ African-American
    ___ Caribbean

___ Caucasian/White

___ Latino/Hispanic
    ___ Central American
    ___ Cuban
    ___ Mexican
    ___ Puerto Rican
    ___ South American

___ Native American

___ Mixed Ethnicity

___ Other

V. Population Served by the Collaborative Program

A. Is your collaborative:
    ___ In the planning stages for providing direct services?
    ___ Currently providing direct services?
    ___ Neither of the above? (If you check this option, please skip to Section VI)

For the following questions on the population served, please give us your best projection for the first year of service delivery if your collaborative is still in the planning phase. If your collaborative program is currently providing services, please give the best estimates for the past year.

B. Please estimate to the best of your ability how many are (will be) served annually by your collaborative program. Use whichever category applies:
    ___ Children/Youth
    ___ Individuals
    ___ Families

C. What is the age of the population your collaborative (will) serve or target?
(CHECK ALL AGE GROUPS THAT APPLY)

___ Family (all ages)
___ Infants/Toddlers (0-3)
___ Preschool (4-5)
___ Early Childhood (0-5)
___ Elementary/Children (6-10)
___ Middle School/Young Adolescents (11-13)
___ High School/Adolescents (14-18)
___ All Children (0-18)
___ Young Adults (19-24)
___ Adults

D. Of the people served by the program each year, estimate the percentage who are (will be)
___ Female? % ___ Male?%

E. Please estimate what percentage of the children and families (to be) served by your collaborative program fall into each of the following racial/ethnic groups: (Note that the percentage for each major category should be the sum of the sub-categories. For example, if your program serves 10% Central Americans and 15% Mexican Americans, the total Hispanic/Latino percentage should be 25%) If you do not have information about the sub-categories, leave them blank.

____% Asian/Pacific Islander
    ____% Cambodian
    ____% Chinese
    ____% Hmong
    ____% Indian
    ____% Japanese
    ____% Korean
    ____% Pacific Islander
    ____% Vietnamese
    ____% Other

____% Black
    ____% African
    ____% African-American
    ____% Caribbean

____% Caucasian/White

____% Latino/Hispanic
    ____% Central American
    ____% Cuban
    ____% Mexican
    ____% Puerto Rican
    ____% South American

____% Native American

____% Mixed Ethnicity

____% Other

F. Please estimate how many of the people your collaborative (will) serve are immigrants/foreign-born:
___ None
___ Less than a quarter
___ Between one quarter and one half
___ Between one-half and three-quarters
___ More than three-quarters
___ All

G. What languages do the people you (will) serve speak? (CHECK ALL THAT APPLY)
__ Armenian
__ Cambodian
__ Chinese (Cantonese, Mandarin, other dialect)
__ English
__ Filipino/Tagalog
__ French
__ Hmong
__ Korean
__ Russian
__ Spanish
__ Vietnamese
__ Other

H. Please estimate how many of the children/youth you (will) serve have difficulty communicating in English because they speak another language:
__ None
__ Less than a quarter
__ Between one quarter and one half
__ Between one-half and three-quarters
__ More than three-quarters
__ All

I. Please estimate how many of the parents you (will) serve have difficulty communicating in English because they speak another language:
__ None
__ Less than a quarter
__ Between one quarter and one half
__ Between one-half and three-quarters
__ More than three-quarters
__ All

J. Are the majority of the families (who will be) served by your collaborative program living in poverty?
__ Yes __ No

VI. Funding for the Collaborative Program

This section asks for funding information. If you are unsure about the funding sources for your collaborative efforts, please indicate an individual who would know the details whom we should contact and skip to Section VII. of this survey:

Name: _____ Telephone: _____

Title: _____

Please indicate with a check each of the sources of funding for your collaborative program (not your agency). Does any of the funding for your collaborative program come from:

A. Private funding
    __ No (SKIP TO B)
    __ Foundations
    __ Corporations/Businesses
    __ United Way
    __ Voluntary Organizations
    __ Individual Donations
    __ Other

B. Public funding
    __ No public funding (SKIP TO C)

    __ FEDERAL
        __ Carl Perkins Vocational Education Act
        __ Community Development Block Grant
        __ Child Care Block Grant
        __ Job Training Partnership Act (JTPA)
        __ McKinney Act
        __ Title IVB (Child Welfare)
        __ Title IVE (Child Welfare Preventive)
        __ Title IVF (JOBS)
        __ Title VII (Education)
        __ Title XIX (Medicaid)
        __ Title XX (Social Services Block Grant)
        __ P.L. 99-457 Part H (SED)
        __ Chapter One (Education)
        __ Chapter Two (Education)
        __ Other

    __ STATE (Only California programs need respond):
        __ SB620
        __ SB910
        __ AFLP
        __ Family Preservation (558/546)
        __ SB65
        __ Other

    __ CITY

    __ COUNTY

    __ SCHOOL DISTRICT

    __ TOWNSHIP

    __ OTHER

C. What is your collaborative program's total annual budget? Please include funding from ALL sources both private and public. [Do NOT include in-kind contributions, including professional staff.]

$_____ Year_____

D. Does your collaborative receive in-kind support from participating agencies?
Please check all categories that apply:

__ Professional staff   __ Clerical support
__ Office spaceUtilities   __ Office supplies

__ Other_____

VII. Other Information

A. California Tomorrow often shares information with the Family Resource Coalition and the National Center for Service Integration. May we pass on this survey information to these two groups? ___Yes ___No

B. May staff members from the Family Resource Coalition and the National Center for Service Integration contact you if they have further questions?

__ Yes __No

C. Is your organization willing to accept requests from the general public for information on its programs?

__ Yes __ Yes, but on a limited basis __ No

D. Would your organization provide technical assistance to those wishing to start a similar program?

__ Yes (PLEASE ANSWER 'E' BELOW)
__ No

E. Do you charge a fee for this technical assistance service?

__ Yes __No

F. Please feel free to attach any materials about your organization and programs which would help us better understand what you do.

G. Comments:

_____

_____

_____

_____

_____

_____

_____

Thank you for taking the time to fill out this survey.

DATE SURVEY COMPLETED:_____

APPENDIX C
Select Bibliography

Anderson, Penny P. and Emily Schrag Fenichel. *Serving Culturally Diverse Families of Infants and Toddlers With Disabilities*. National Center for Clinical Infant Programs, Washington, D.C., 1989.

Arcia, Emily et. al. *Status of Young Mexican American and Puerto Rican Children: Implications for Early Intervention Systems*. University of North Carolina, Chapel Hill, February 1993.

Barnett, Kevin. "Collaboration for Community Empowerment: Re-defining the Role of Academic Institutions, Developing New Partnerships to Improve Community Quality of Life." Center for Community Health, School of Public Health, University of California, Berkeley, 1993.

Barr, Don and Moncrieff Cochran. "Understanding and Supporting Empowerment: Redefining the Professional Role." *Empowerment and Family Support Networking Bulletin*, Vol. 2, Issue 3 (June 1992).

Berger, Ruth. "Promoting Minority Access to the Profession." *Social Work*, Vol. 34, No. 4 (1989).

Bruner, Charles, et. al. "Charting a Course: Assessing a Community's Strengths and Needs." National Center for Service Integration Resource Brief 2. National Center for Service Integration, New York, NY, 1993.

Building Strong Communities. Conference Report sponsored by the Anne E. Casey, Ford and Rockefeller Foundations. Cleveland, Ohio, May 13-15, 1992.

California Department of Education. *Handbook for Teaching Korean-American Students*. Bilingual Education Office, Sacramento, CA, 1992.

Chang, Hedy Nai-Lin. "Diversity: The Essential Link in Collaborative Services." *California Perspectives*, Vol. 4 (Fall 1992).

Child Welfare League of America. *CWLA Initiative to Promote Culturally Responsive Child Welfare Practice*. Washington, D.C., 1990.

Cochran, Moncrieff. "Parent Empowerment: Developing A Conceptual Framework." *Family Science Review*, Vol. 5, No. 1 & 2 (February and May 1992).

Comer, J.P. "Educating Poor Minority Children." *Scientific American*, Vol. 259, No. 5. (1988).

Cummins, Jim. "Empowering Minority Students: A Framework for Intervention." *Harvard Educational Review*, Vol. 56, No. 1 (1986).

Dezerotes, David S. and Lonnie R. Snowden. "Cultural Factors in the Intervention of Child Maltreatment." *Social Service Review*, Vol. 7, No. 2 (1990).

Dolinsky, Arthur L., Richard K. Casputo and Patrick O'Kane. "Competing Effects of Culture and Situation on Welfare Receipt." *Social Service Review*, Vol. 63, No. 3 (1990).

Gutierrez, Lorraine M. "Working With Women of Color: An Empowerment Perspective." *Social Work* (March 1990).

Hall, Ethel H. and Gloria C. King. "Working With the Strengths of Black Families." *Child Welfare*, Vol. LXI, No. 8 (1982).

Himmelman, Arthur Turovh. "Communities Working Collaboratively for a Change." Minneapolis, MN: The Himmelman Consulting Group (1992).

Hirayama, Hisashi and Muammer Cetingok. "Empowerment: A Social Work Approach for Asian Immigrants." *Social Casework* (January 1988).

Ho, M.K.. "Social Work with Asian Americans." *Social Casework*, Vol. 57, No. 3 (1976).

Hodges, Vanessa G. "Providing Culturally Sensitive Intensive Family Preservation Services to Ethnic Minority Families." In *Intensive Family Preservation Services: An Instructional Handbook*, edited by Elizabeth M. Tracy et. al. Mandell School of Applied Social Sciences, Case Western Reserve University, Cleveland, OH, 1991.

Hogan, Patricia Turner and Sau-Fong Su. "Minority Children and the Child Welfare System: A Historical Perspective." *Social Work*, Vol. 33, No. 6 (1988).

Hong, George K. and Lawrence K. Hong. "Comparative Perspectives on Child Abuse and Neglect: Chinese versus Hispanics and Whites." *Child Welfare*, Vol. LXX, No. 4 (1991).

Huey, John. "Finding New Heroes For A New Era." *Fortune Magazine*, (January 25, 1993).

Ifill, Don. "Teaching Minority Practice for Professional Application." *Journal of Social Work Education*, Vol. 25, No. 1 (1989).

Ignacio, L.F. "The Pacific/Asian Coalition: Origin, Structure and Program."
Social Casework, Vol. 57, No. 3 (1976).

Institute for Educational Leadership. *Framework for Systems Reform.*
Washington D.C., 1994.

Institute for Social Change, U.C. Berkeley. *The Diversity Project: Final Report.*
November 1991.

Jones, E.E. and A. Thorne. "Rediscovery of the Subject: Intercultural Approaches
to Clinical Assessment." *Journal of Consulting and Clinical Psychology*,
Vol. 55, No. 4 (1987).

Katlin, Fay. "The Impact of Ethnicity." *Social Casework*, Vol. 63, No. 3 (1982).

Keller, Gordon N. "Bicultural Social Work and Anthropology." *Social Casework*,
Vol. 52, No. 8 (1972).

Kim, Bok-Lim C. "An Appraisal of Korean Immigrant Service Needs."
Social Casework, Vol. 57, No. 3 (1976).

Kretzmann, John P. and John L. McKnight. *Building Communities From The Inside Out:
A Path Toward Finding And Mobilizing A Community's Assets.* Center for Urban
Affairs and Policy Research Neighborhood Innovation Network, Northwestern
University, Evanston, IL, 1993.

Lee, Evelyn. *Cultural Competence Training Handbook.* Ventura County Health Care
Agency, Ventura, CA, 1992.

Lewis, Sylvia. "America's Cities: What Works, Tough Love Works in Newark."
Planning (October 1993).

Lott, J.T. "Migration of a Mentality: The Philipino Community." *Social Casework*,
Vol. 57, No. 3 (1976).

Lynch, Eleanor W. and Marci J. Hanson. *Developing Cross-Cultural Competence:
A Guide for Working with Young Children and Their Families.* Paul H. Brookes
Publishing Co., Baltimore, MD, 1992.

Mass, A.I. "Asians as Individuals: The Japanese Community." *Social Casework*,
Vol. 57, No. 3 (1976).

McKelvy, Doris. "Agency Change: A Response to the Needs of Black Families and
Children." *Child Welfare*, Vol. LX, No. 3 (1981).

McNeely, Joseph B. "Building for the Future: A Discussion Paper on Strengthening Staff Leadership in Community-Based Development Organizations." Fannie Mae Foundation, Washington, D.C., 1993.

Melaville, Atelia I., Martin J. Blank, and Gelareh Asayesh. *Together We Can: A Guide for Crafting a Profamily System of Education and Human Services.* Office of Educational Research and Improvement, U.S. Department of Education, and Office of the Assistant Secretary for Planning and Evaluation, U.S. Department of Health and Human Services, Washington, D.C. April 1993.

Myers, Michael, T. "The African-American Experience With HIV Disease," *Focus: A Guide to AIDS Research and Counseling.* Vol. 7, No. 4 (March 1992).

Morris, Teresa M. "Culturally Sensitive Family Assesment: An Evaluation of the Family Assesment Device Used With Hawaiian-American and Japanese-American Families." *Family Process,* Vol. 29 (1990).

Mostwin, D. "In Search of Ethnic Identity." *Social Casework,* Vol. 53, No. 5 (1972).

Neugebauer, Bonnie, ed. *Alike and Different: Exploring Our Humanity with Young Children.* National Association for the Education of Young Children, Washington, D.C., 1992.

Oliver, John and Lester B. Brown. "The Development and Implementation of a Minority Recruitment Plan: Process, Strategy and Results." *Journal of Social Work Education,* Vol. 24, No. 2 (1988).

Olsen, Laurie. "Mission Imperative." *California Perspectives,* Vol. 3 (Fall 1992).

Olsen, Laurie, et. al. *The Unfinished Journey: Restructuring Schools in a Diverse Society.* California Tomorrow, San Francisco, January 1994.

Opening Unlocked Doors: A National Agenda for Ensuring Quality Education for Children and Youth in Low-Income Public Housing and Other Low-Income Residential Communities. Quality Education for Minorities (QEM) Network, Washington, D.C., 1993.

Paviour, Robert. "The Influence of Class and Race on Clinical Assessments by MSW Students." *Social Service Review,* Vol. 62, No. 4 (1988).

Pinderhughes, Elaine. *Understanding Race, Ethnicity, and Power: the Key to Efficacy in Clinical Practice.* The Free Press, New York, NY, 1989.

Potapchuk, William R. and Margaret A. Bailey. *Building the Collaborative Community: A Select Bibliography for Community Leaders.* Program for Community Problem Solving, Washington, D.C., 1992.

Randall-David, Elizabeth. *Strategies for Working With Culturally Diverse Communities and Clients.* The Association for the Care of Children's Health, Washington, D.C., 1989.

Ruben, B.D. "The Study of Cross-Cultural Competence: Traditions and Contemporary Issues." *International Journal of Intercultural Relations*, Vol. 13 (1989).

Schneller, R. "Intercultural and Intrapersonal Processes and Factors of Misunderstanding: Implications for Multicultural Training." *International Journal of Intercultural Relations*, Vol. 13 (1989).

Schoene Jr., Lester P. and Marcelle E. DuPraw. *Facing Racial and Cultural Conflict: Tools for Rebuilding Community.* Program for Community Problem Solving, Washington, D.C., 1992.

Simons, George F. *Working Together: How to Become More Effective in a Multicultural Organization.* Crisp Publications, Inc., Los Altos, CA, 1989.

Stehno, Sandra M. "The Elusive Continuum of Child Welfare Services: Implications for Minority Children and Youth." *Child Welfare*, Vol. LXIX, No. 6 (1990).

Suchman, Diane R. "Turning Around Inner-City Neighborhoods." *Urban Land*, (September 1993).

California Tomorrow Publications

Affirming Children's Roots:
Cultural and Linguistic Diversity in Early Care and Education

$17.00, 101 pages

What are the implications of cultural and ethnic diversity for early care and education? This new report presents findings of research documenting the impact of California's demographic changes on child care centers. It explores questions about the implications of our growing diversity for early care and education through a review of the literature and profiles of sites and training programs in California. Includes recommendations for policy and practice, and an annotated bibliography.

Bridges:
Promising Programs for the Education of Immigrant Children

$17.00, 175 pages.

A resource for educators and advocates concerned with the education of immigrant youth and their transition to U.S. schools and culture. Described 75 working programs at the school, district and community levels, with contact names and addresses: newcomer schools, intake and assessment centers, counseling and transition support, intercultural relations, immigrant parent outreach, curricula, supplementary academic supports, teacher training and technological innovations. Bibliography of literature, films and curricula.

California Perspectives:
An Anthology from California Tomorrow's Education for a Diverse Society Project, Vol. 2, 1991

$12.00, 58 pages.

Includes articles, "Stopping Bias in its Tracks," on Cabrillo Community College's Anti-Bias Curriculum course that teaches early childhood professionals to help young people combat prejudice; journals of student teachers working in diverse classrooms; an analysis of California's debate over the social studies curriculum and the broader issues of power, knowledge and national identity; two women's experiences growing up biracial and bicultural, and more.

California Perspectives:
An Anthology from California Tomorrow, Vol. 3, 1992

$15.00, 82 pages

A collection of thought-provoking essays, this journal offers insights into the forces shaping our course as the nation's most multiethnic state. Topics range from the movement to create African-centered education to how the growing anti-immigrant sentiment and misinformation regarding immigrant uses of public services threatens our future.

The Children Nobody Knows:
California's Foster Care-Dependency System

$12.00, 108 pages.

Based on five years of research, this report chronicles California's exploding foster care system and analyzes emergency shelters, judicial proceedings, family reunification programs, and the demographics, health and emotional status of foster children, the majority of whom are ethnic minorities. Features interviews with children and social workers, policy recommendations, charts and statistics.

Crossing the Schoolhouse Border:
Immigrant Students in the California Public Schools

$16.00, 128 pages.

A groundbreaking report based on interviews with more than 400 immigrant students and hundreds of educators, community workers and parents about the needs and experiences of newcomers in California's classrooms. Information about the backgrounds of the students, their academic and social needs and adjustments, the political climate and funding.

Drawing Strength from Diversity:
Effective Services for Children, Youth and Families

Further copies may be purchased for $21 plus sales tax at the address below.

Embracing Diversity:
Teachers' Voices from California Classrooms

$20.00, 115 pages

Meet 36 California teachers doing remarkable work in mainstream classrooms with students of diverse cultural, national and linguistic backgrounds. Through in-depth interviews, the educators share their strategies to inspire their students to bridge the gaps of language, culture and national backgrounds which often separate them. The teachers send out an urgent call to policymakers, staff developers and teacher trainers to support and prepare teachers for the reality of California's diverse classrooms.

Fighting Fragmentation:
Collaborative Efforts to Serve Children and Families in California's Counties

$12.00, 58 pages.

Budget-strapped counties are moving to build new forms of collaboration among agencies that serve children and families with complex needs. This California Tomorrow report documents 31 such efforts among schools, health providers, businesses, police, courts, social services, parents and others. Based on the premise that fragmentation of services hurts children, *Fighting Fragmentation* includes an analysis of the recent realignment of fiscal responsibility from the state to the county level and its implications for improving services to children and families. Also includes a checklist for a successful collaborative, a bibliography and county-by-county descriptions.

Newcomer Programs
$15.00, 57 pages

This report comprehensively describes special immigrant/newcomer schools and programs from separate-site newcomer schools to half-day programs on regular school sites. *Newcomer Programs* lays out key design and model characteristics of this rapidly proliferating school intervention. Legal and ethical concerns over the separation of immigrant youth and the needs for information-sharing mechanisms among districts are also addressed.

The Unfinished Journey:
Restructuring Schools in a Diverse Society

$27.00, 360 pages

A major new report on school restructuring and reform in California, one of the most active school reform movements in the nation today. *The Unfinished Journey* is about teachers, school principals, parents, and community members who see that the old ways of schooling aren't working for many students, and so they dare to try to invent better ones in their place. The challenge is to seize the opportunity presented by the current school restructuring movement, and to focus creativity and energy upon addressing the challenges of diversity.

California Tomorrow Magazine

Back issues available of this acclaimed journal published from 1986-1990, including special issues on mental health, the environment, and the 1990 Census. Please write for index and prices.

Ordering Information

Please add sales tax when ordering publications. Discounts of 20% available on orders of 10 or more copies of the same title. Please mail order requests to:

California Tomorrow
Fort Mason Center
Building B
San Francisco, CA 94123